Skills Link™

Everyday
Mathematics®

D0661237

Skills Link™

Everyday
Mathematics®

Cumulative Practice Sets

A Division of The McGraw·Hill Companies

Columbus, Ohio
Chicago, Illinois

Photo Credits

Cover–Bill Burlingham/Photography
Photo Collage–Herman Adler Design

www.sra4kids.com

SRA/McGraw-Hill

A Division of The McGraw-Hill Companies

Send all inquiries to:
SRA/McGraw-Hill
P.O. Box 812960
Chicago, IL 60681

Printed in the United States of America.

ISBN 1-57039-941-7

8 9 10 11 12 13 VHG 07 06 05 04 03

Contents

Write all of your answers on a separate sheet of paper.

Find the missing number.

1.

	598	
607		609

2.

24		26
44		46

3.

179
199

4.

	707
	717
	727

5.
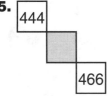

444	
	466

6.

998	999	

7. Put these numbers in order from least to greatest:
259   262   260   258   263   261

8. Put these numbers in order from greatest to least:
990   980   1,000   1,100   970   1,200

Count by 2s. Find the missing numbers.

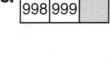

Unit
socks

9. 31, 33, ■, ■, ■, 41, ■, ■, ■, 49

10. 92, ■, 96, ■, 100, ■, ■, 106, ■, ■

11. 131, 133, ■, ■, 139, ■, ■, 145, ■, ■

Practice Set 2

Record the time shown on each clock.

Write your answers on a separate sheet of paper.

1.

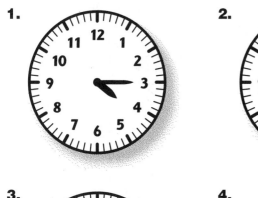

2.

3.

4.

5.

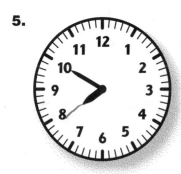

6.

Use with or after Lesson 1.4.

Write all of your answers on a separate sheet of paper.

7. Measure the above line segment in inches.

8. Now measure it in centimeters.

Write the name of each shape.

9.   **10.**    **11.**

12. 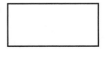   **13.**   **14.**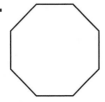

15.   **16.**   **17.**

Write all of your answers on a separate sheet of paper.

Use the tally chart to answer each question below.

Ice Cream Favorites	
Kind of Ice Cream	**Number of Students**
Vanilla	ЖЖ
Strawberry	ЖЖ //
Double Chocolate	ЖЖ ЖЖ //
Chocolate Chip Mint	////
Maple Nut	///

1. How many students like Double Chocolate ice cream best?

2. What is the favorite flavor?

3. What is the least-favorite flavor?

4. How many students altogether chose Double Chocolate or Chocolate Chip Mint?

Write the number shown by the base-10 blocks.

5.

6.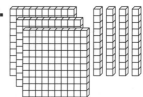

7.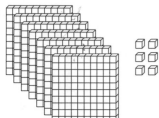

8.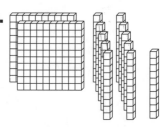

Use with or after Lesson 1.5.

Use the bar graph to answer each question below.

Write your answers on a separate sheet of paper.

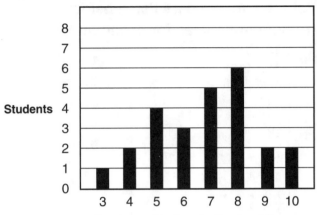

Students

Numbers of Letters in Our Last Names

9. How many students have eight letters in their last names?

10. How many letters are in the *shortest* last name?

11. How many names are shown by the bar graph?

12. How many students have fewer than six letters in their last names?

13. How many letters does the *longest* name have? (This is called the *maximum.*)

14. How many letters does the *shortest* name have? (This is called the *minimum.*)

15. What is the *range* of the numbers of letters?

16. What is the *mode* of this set of data?

(*Hint:* If you don't remember what range and mode are, look them up in your *Student Reference Book.*)

Write all of your answers on a separate sheet of paper.

**Make up your own name-collection box
for each of the five numbers listed below.
Include 10 different names for each number.**

Example

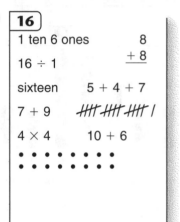

1. 9
2. 14
3. 8
4. 12
5. 10

6. Count by 3s
3, 6, 9, 12, ■, ■, ■, ■, ■, ■

Unit
shoes

7. Count back by 10s.
140, 130, 120, ■, ■, ■, ■, ■, ■

Add.

8. $7 + 8 = $ ■ **9.** $6 + 9 = $ ■ **10.** $9 + 5 = $ ■

11. $12 + 8 = $ ■ **12.** $6 + 8 = $ ■ **13.** $8 + 9 = $ ■

Practice Set 5

Write all of your answers on a separate sheet of paper.

									0
1	2	3	4	5	6	7	8	9	10
11	12	13	14	15	16	17	18	19	20
21	22	23	24	25	26	27	28	29	30
31	32	33	34	35	36	37	38	39	40
41	42	43	44	45	46	47	48	49	50
51	52	53	54	55	56	57	58	59	60
61	62	63	64	65	66	67	68	69	70
71	72	73	74	75	76	77	78	79	80
81	82	83	84	85	86	87	88	89	90
91	92	93	94	95	96	97	98	99	100
101	102	103	104	105	106	107	108	109	110

1. Find 20 more than 84.　　**2.** Find 16 more than 68.

3. Find 12 less than 32.　　**4.** Find 35 less than 44.

5. Start at 0 and count by 3s along the *second* line of the number grid. Write the numbers from your count.

6. Start at 41 and count by 3s along the *sixth* line of the number grid. Write the numbers from your count.

7. Start at 81 and count by 6s along *two lines* of the number grid. Write the numbers from your count.

Write all of your answers on a separate sheet of paper.

Use your calculator to count by 10s.
Find the missing numbers.

> **Example** 40, ■, ■, 70, 80, ■, ■
>
> **Press:** ④ ⓪ ⊕ ① ⓪ ⊜ ⊜ ⊜ ⊜ ⊜ ⊜
>
> **Display:** 50, 60, 70, 80, 90, 100

1. 25, ■, 45, ■, ■, ■, 85, ■, ■, ■

2. 123, ■, 143, ■, ■, ■, ■, ■, ■, 213

Use your calculator to solve each problem.

3. The first English colony was established in the New World in 1607. The colonies united to demand freedom from England in 1776. How many years went by before the colonies demanded freedom?

4. Marta read a book that was 45 pages long. Next, she read a book that was 82 pages long. Then she read a book that was 106 pages long. How many pages did Marta read in all?

Write the missing numbers.

Unit
books

5. 10 = ■ + 4   **6.** 5 + ■ = 10

7. ■ + 7 = 10   **8.** 26 + ■ = 30

9. 50 = ■ + 43   **10.** 81 + ■ = 90

Write all of your answers on a separate sheet of paper.

Estimate to answer *yes* or *no*.

1. You have $5.00. Do you have enough to buy a notebook for $3.99 and a pen for $1.55?

2. You have $4.50. Do you have enough to buy two boxes of pencils that cost $2.10 each?

3. You have $10.00. Do you have enough to buy crayons for $1.89, a backpack for $6.98, and paper clips for 79¢?

4. You have $3.20. Do you have enough to buy a marker for $1.79 and a pad of paper for $1.49?

Solve each problem.

5. Juana paid for a video that cost $6.59 with a $10.00 bill. How much change did she receive?

6. Larry's lunch cost $3.25. Larry paid for his lunch with a $5.00 bill. How much change did he receive?

Find an equal amount of money in the second list. Then write the letter that identifies that amount.

7. $\frac{1}{2}$ dime

8. quarter

9. $\frac{1}{10}$ dollar

10. $0.01

11. $\frac{1}{2}$ dollar

12. $0.75

A. dime

B. $0.50

C. $\frac{3}{4}$ dollar

D. penny

E. nickel

F. $\frac{1}{4}$ dollar

Write all of your answers on a separate sheet of paper.

Write =, <, or >.

> = means *is equal to*
> < means *is less than*
> > means *is greater than*

13. $1.59 ■ $0.95

14. $7.52 ■ $4.75

15. $0.88 ■ $1.08

16. $6.65 ■ $5.66

17. $10.01 ■ $9.10   **18.** $0.75 ■ 75 cents

19. $1.11 ■ 111 pennies   **20.** 63 cents ■ $1.63

Use your calculator. Enter each amount of money.
Then write the equivalent numeric value
that is displayed on your calculator.

Example   Enter: 93¢   Display shows: 0.93

21. $0.08   **22.** $1.59   **23.** 98¢   **24.** $6.57

25. 3¢   **26.** 59¢   **27.** $2.43   **28.** $0.79

Draw coins to show each amount of money
in two different ways.

Example   87¢

29. 42¢   **30.** $0.35   **31.** 27¢

32. $0.54   **33.** 68¢   **34.** 76¢

Write all of your answers on a separate sheet of paper.

Complete each Frames-and-Arrows diagram.

Example

Rule
Add 2

14 16 18 20 22

1.

Rule
+ 10

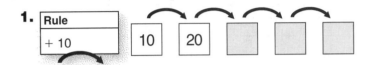

10 20 ▢ ▢ ▢

2.

Rule
− 2

28 26 ⬡ ⬡ ⬡

3.

Rule
Subtract 10

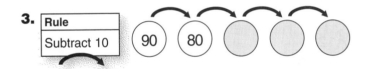

90 80 ◯ ◯ ◯

Find each missing number.

4. 1 Ⓠ = ■ ¢

5. 20 Ⓟ = ■ ¢

6. ■ Ⓓ = $0.60

7. ■ Ⓠ = $1

8. 1 half-dollar = ■ ¢

9. ■ Ⓠ = 10 Ⓝ

10. 1 quarter = ■ dimes and ■ nickels

11. ■ dimes and ■ pennies = 1 dollar

Write all of your answers on a separate sheet of paper.

Write the number family for each Fact Triangle.

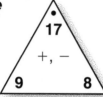

Example

$9 + 8 = 17$
$8 + 9 = 17$
$17 - 9 = 8$
$17 - 8 = 9$

1.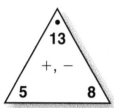

2.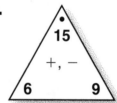

3.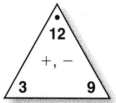

4.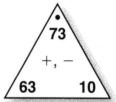

Write the addition and subtraction number family for each group of numbers.

Example 7, 14, 7	$7 + 7 = 14$
	$14 - 7 = 7$

5. 8, 8, 16   **6.** 9, 9, 18

7. 20, 20, 40   **8.** 28, 14, 14

9. 30, 30, 60   **10.** 36, 18, 18

Use with or after Lesson 2.1.

Use two rules for each set of Frames and Arrows.
Write the numbers for the empty frames. (Write your
answers on a separate sheet of paper.)

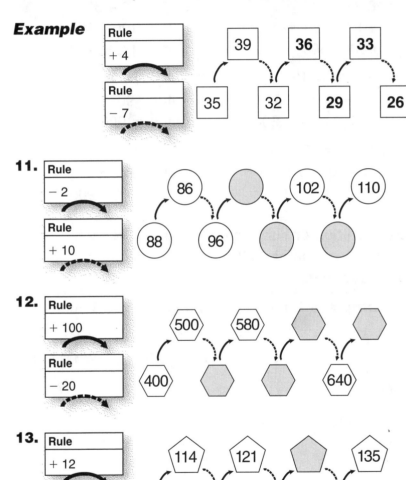

Example

Rule
+ 4

Rule
− 7

39   36   33

35   32   29   26

11.

Rule
− 2

Rule
+ 10

86   ( )   102   110

88   96   ( )   ( )

12.

Rule
+ 100

Rule
− 20

500   580   ( )   ( )

400   ( )   ( )   640

13.

Rule
+ 12

Rule
− 5

114   121   ( )   135

102   ( )   ( )   ( )

Practice Set 10

Write all of your answers on a separate sheet of paper.

Find each missing number.

1. $6 + 8 = $ ■
$60 + 80 = $ ■
$600 + 800 = $ ■

2. ■ $= 12 - 5$
■ $= 120 - 50$
■ $= 1,200 - 500$

3. $9 + $ ■ $= 13$
$90 + $ ■ $= 130$
$900 + $ ■ $= 1,300$

4. $4 = 9 - $ ■
$40 = 90 - $ ■
$400 = 900 - $ ■

5. ■ $- 8 = 7$
■ $- 80 = 70$
■ $- 800 = 700$

6. $8 = $ ■ $- 9$
$80 = $ ■ $- 90$
$800 = $ ■ $- 900$

Use addition or subtraction to complete each problem on your calculator. Tell how much you added or subtracted.

Example	Enter 34	Change to 50	What I did + 16

	Enter	Change to	What I did
7.	90	72	?
8.	22	50	?
9.	100	58	?
10.	200	120	?
11.	130	250	?
12.	900	400	?

Use with or after Lesson 2.2.

Write the names that DO NOT belong in each name-collection box. (Write your answers on a separate sheet of paper.)

Example

15

5 less than 19

5 × 3

4 × 4   8 + 6

3 + 3 + 3 + 3 + 3

7 + 6 + 3   ~~HHT~~ ~~HHT~~ ~~HHT~~

5 + 5 + 5

2 more than 13

Names that DO NOT belong:

5 less than 19

8 + 6

7 + 6 + 3

4 × 4

13.

16

six   4   9
         × 4   × 2

16 × 1

10 + 6   3 × 5

6 + 6 + 5

2 more than 14

3 less than 20

14.

14

15 − 1   7
           + 7

14 + 1

0 + 14   • • • • • • •

7 × 7   • • • • • • •

5 + 4 + 6   ~~HHT~~ ~~HHT~~ ////

9 + 6   10 + 4

15.

12

12 + 1   3
           × 4

20 − 8

3 + 10   1 × 12

5 + 8   2 × 6

• • •   ~~HHT~~ ///
• • •
• • •
• • •

16.

20

twenty   4 × 5

~~HHT~~ ~~HHT~~ ~~HHT~~ ////

13 + 8   twenty

20 + 0

5 + 6 + 9   10 + 10

20 × 0

8 + 7 + 7

Find each missing number. (Write your answers on a separate sheet of paper.)

Example

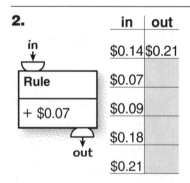

in	out
6	11
9	*14*
3	*8*
15	*20*
11	*16*

1.

in	out
15	9
10	
17	
21	
30	

Rule −6

2.

in	out
$0.14	$0.21
$0.07	
$0.09	
$0.18	
$0.21	

Rule + $0.07

3.

in	out
5	10
6	
10	
12	
15	

Rule Double

Choose one of the diagrams to help you solve
each number story below.

Write all of your answers on a separate sheet of paper.

1. Bedelia picked 23 flowers
Tuesday. She picked more
flowers Wednesday. She
picked a total of 47 flowers.
How many flowers did
she pick Wednesday?
Answer the question:

_____

Number model: _____

Quantity

Quantity	Difference

Total

Part	Part

Start	Change	End

2. Sara spelled 83 words
correctly at this year's
spelling contest. Last year
she spelled only 47 words
correctly. What is the difference
between her two scores?
Answer the question:

_____

Number model: _____

3. Larissa made 67 paper birds
for a crafts fair. Then she made
38 paper insects. How many
objects did she make in all?
Answer the question:

_____

Number model: _____

Practice Set 12 (cont.)

Write all of your answers on a separate sheet of paper.

Count by 10s. Find the missing numbers.

4. 400; 410; ■; 430; ■; ■; 460; ■; ■; ■; 500

5. 1,010; 1,020; ■; 1,040; ■; ■; 1,070; ■; ■; 1,100

6. 3,225; 3,235; ■; ■; 3,265; ■; ■; ■; 3,305; ■

7. 8,712; 8,722; ■; 8,742; ■; ■; 8,772; ■; ■; 8,802

8. 3,218; 3,228; ■; ■; 3,258; ■; ■; ■; 3,298; ■

**Tell what the underlined digit stands for
in each number.**

Example 9,<u>6</u>13   **6 hundreds, or 600**

9. <u>2</u>,917   **10.** 3,04<u>6</u>   **11.** 8<u>5</u>1

12. 8,<u>0</u>46   **13.** <u>5</u>,425   **14.** <u>1</u>4,523

15. 6,79<u>1</u>   **16.** 4,3<u>8</u>0   **17.** 6<u>3</u>,941

**Write the addition and subtraction number family
for each group of numbers.**

Example 5, 17, 22   5 + 17 = 22
17 + 5 = 22
22 − 5 = 17
22 − 17 = 5

18. 28, 9, 37   **19.** 50, 30, 80   **20.** 6, 57, 63

21. 60, 8, 52   **22.** 70, 90, 160   **23.** 400, 500, 900

Estimate first. Then use the partial-sums addition method to add.

Write all of your answers on a separate sheet of paper.

Example

100s	10s	1s
4	6	7
+	1	8
4	0	0
	7	0
	1	5
4	8	5

Ballpark estimate:

$470 + 20 = 490$

1. 345
     + 69

Ballpark estimate:

_____

2.   38
     + 45

Ballpark estimate:

_____

3.   75
     + 129

Ballpark estimate:

_____

Estimate first. Then use the trade-first subtraction method to subtract.

Write all of your answers on a separate sheet of paper.

Example

100s	10s	1s
/	/2	
2̸	2̸	5
− 1	7	3
	5	2

Ballpark estimate:

$225 - 175 = 50$

---

1. 305
  − 69

Ballpark estimate:

_____

---

2. 138
  − 45

Ballpark estimate:

_____

3. 275
  − 129

Ballpark estimate:

_____

Write all of your answers on a separate sheet of paper.

Find each missing number.

4. $1 = ■Ⓓ

5. $0.42 = ■Ⓟ

6. ■ half-dollars = $2.00

7. ■Ⓝ = 4Ⓓ

8. 75¢ = ■Ⓠ

9. ■Ⓓ = 1 half-dollar

10. ■Ⓝ = 35¢

11. $0.70 = ■Ⓓ

Add or subtract.

Unit
fish

12. 52 + 79

13. 98 − 46

14. 14 + 24 + 36

15. 81 − 49

16. 26 + 91

17. 65 − 28

18. 104
− 67

19. 26
+ 13

20. 79
− 24

21. 57
+ 26

Count by 100s. Find the missing numbers.

22. 1,000; 1,100; ■; 1,300; ■; ■; 1,600; ■; ■; 1,900

23. 2,450; 2,550; ■; ■; 2,850; ■; 3,050; ■; ■; 3,350

24. 7,304; 7,404; ■; ■; ■; 7,804; ■; 8,004; ■; ■

25. 5,416; ■; ■; 5,716; ■; ■; ■; 6,116; 6,216; 6,316

26. 2,883; ■; ■; 3,183; 3,283; ■; ■; ■; 3,683; ■

Copy and use one of the diagrams below to help you solve each problem.

Write all of your answers on a separate sheet of paper.

Total		
Part	Part	Part

Total			
Part	Part	Part	Part

1. Samuel bought presents for 40 cents, 50 cents, 60 cents, and 70 cents. How much money did he spend in all?

   Check: Does my answer make sense?

2. Trini rode her bicycle 12 miles Friday. She rode 14 miles Saturday and 15 miles Sunday. How many miles did she ride in all?

   Check: Does my answer make sense?

3. Jon, Dave, and Kevin collected rocks at the beach. Each boy collected 25 rocks. How many rocks did the boys collect in all?

   Check: Does my answer make sense?

4. The Torrey family was on vacation. One day, they spent $140 for a motel room, $130 for meals, and $200 at a park. How much money did they spend that day?

   Check: Does my answer make sense?

Copy each Addition and Subtraction Puzzle on a separate sheet of paper. Then find the missing numbers.

Example

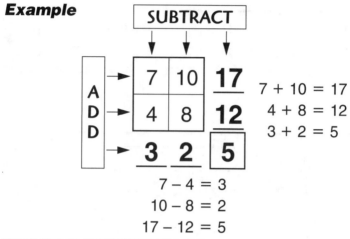

SUBTRACT		
7	10	**17**
4	8	**12**
3	**2**	**5**

A D D

$7 + 10 = 17$
$4 + 8 = 12$
$3 + 2 = 5$

$7 - 4 = 3$
$10 - 8 = 2$
$17 - 12 = 5$

5.

SUBTRACT

A D D

35	29	
18	15	

6.

SUBTRACT

A D D

53	34	
39	21	

7.

SUBTRACT

A D D

	75	
		15
25	**70**	

8.

SUBTRACT

A D D

84		**137**
64		
		56

Measure each line segment to the nearest $\frac{1}{4}$ inch.

Write your answers on a separate sheet of paper.

1.

2.

3.

4.

5.

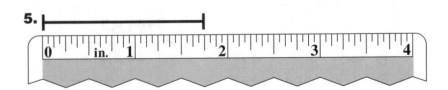

Use with or after Lesson 3.2.

Find the missing number for each Fact Triangle.
Then write the family of facts for that triangle on a
separate sheet of paper.

6.

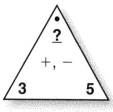

?
+, −
3   5

7.

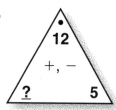

12
+, −
?   5

8.

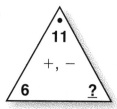

11
+, −
6   ?

9.

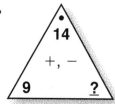

14
+, −
9   ?

10.

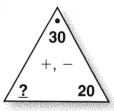

30
+, −
?   20

11.

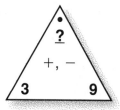

?
+, −
3   9

12.

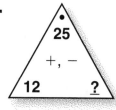

25
+, −
12   ?

13.

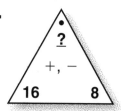

?
+, −
16   8

Write all of your answers on a separate sheet of paper.

Use measuring tools if you need help answering these questions:

1. How many inches in 1 foot?

2. How many inches in 1 yard?

3. How many feet in 1 yard?

4. How many inches in your tape measure?

5. How many centimeters in 1 meter?

6. How many decimeters in 1 meter?

---

7. Draw a line segment that you think is about 7 centimeters long. Then measure it to see how long it actually is.

Measure each line segment to the nearest centimeter.

8.

9.

Find the perimeter of each figure. (Write your answers on a separate sheet of paper.)

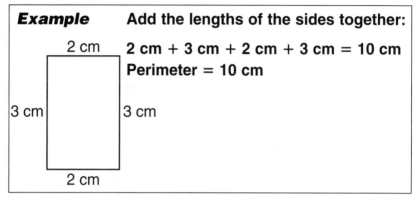

Example — Add the lengths of the sides together:

2 cm

3 cm   3 cm

2 cm

2 cm + 3 cm + 2 cm + 3 cm = 10 cm
Perimeter = 10 cm

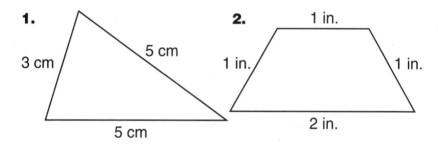

1.

3 cm

5 cm

5 cm

2.

1 in.

1 in.   1 in.

2 in.

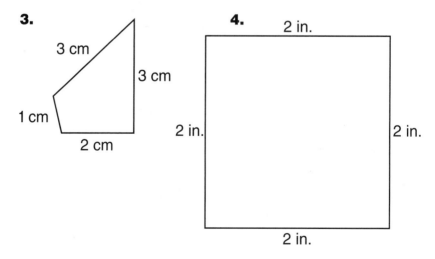

3.

3 cm

3 cm

1 cm

2 cm

4.

2 in.

2 in.   2 in.

2 in.

Write all of your answers on a separate sheet of paper.

Find each sum or difference.

5. 7 + 4
17 + 4
27 + 4
37 + 4
47 + 4

6. 14 − 6
24 − 6
34 − 6
44 − 6
54 − 6

7. 6 + 3
60 + 30
600 + 300

8. 8 − 2
80 − 20
800 − 200

9. 9 + 6
90 + 60
900 + 600

10. 18 − 9
180 − 90
1,800 − 900

Count by 100s. Find the missing numbers.

11. 1,200; 1,100; ■; 900; 800; ■; ■; 500; ■; 300

12. 5,630; 5,530; ■; ■; 5,230; 5,130; ■; 4,930; ■; ■

13. 2,807; ■; 2,607; ■; ■; ■; 2,207; ■; ■; 1,907

14. 7,659; ■; ■; 7,359; ■; ■; ■; 6,959; ■; ■

15. 5,312; 5,212; ■; ■; ■; 4,812; 4,712; ■; ■; ■

Solve each problem.

16. The distance from Dallas to Houston is 245 miles. The distance from Dallas to El Paso is 617 miles. How much farther is it from Dallas to El Paso than from Dallas to Houston?

17. On their vacation, the Baker family drove 376 miles from Phoenix to Los Angeles. Then the Bakers drove 387 miles to San Francisco. How many miles did they drive in all?

Write a number model for each rectangle. Then find the area. (Write your answers on a separate sheet of paper.)

Example	Number model: 3 × 4 = 12
	Area = 12 square units

1.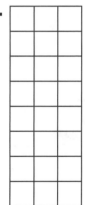

2.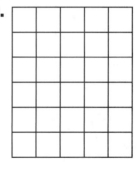

3.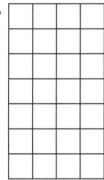

4.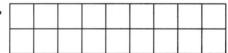

Find the perimeter of each figure. (Write your answers on a separate sheet of paper.)

5.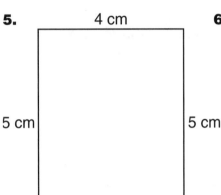
4 cm

5 cm

5 cm

4 cm

6.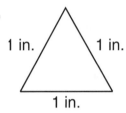
1 in.

1 in.

1 in.

7.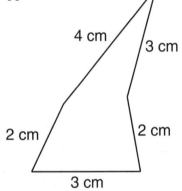
4 cm

3 cm

2 cm

2 cm

3 cm

8.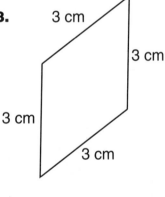
3 cm

3 cm

3 cm

3 cm

9.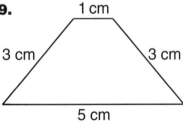
1 cm

3 cm

3 cm

5 cm

10.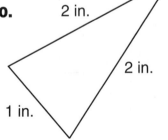
2 in.

2 in.

1 in.

Use with or after Lesson 3.7.

Write all of your answers on a separate sheet of paper.

The diameter is given. Find the circumference by using the "about 3 times" Circle Rule.

1.
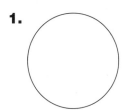

1 in.

2.
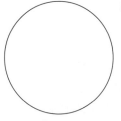

3 cm

3.
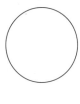

2 cm

Count the bills and coins. Then write the correct amount using dollars-and-cents notation.

4.

5.

6.

7.

Practice Set 21

SRB
167
182–185

Write all of your answers on a separate sheet of paper.

For Problems 1–4, copy the diagram and use it to help you find each answer.

	Units		
Numbers			

1. David has 5 vases. He put 6 flowers in each vase. How many flowers did David put in all of the vases?

2. Sharon bought 4 packs of crackers. Each pack holds 8 crackers. How many crackers did Sharon buy in all?

3. A meeting room has 5 rows of chairs. Each row has 8 chairs. How many chairs are in all of the rows?

4. Each page of a photo album has 4 rows of pictures. Each row has 3 pictures. How many pictures are on each page of the album?

For Problems 5–17, add or subtract. Then make a ballpark estimate to check that your answer makes sense.

Unit
snowballs

5. 112 + 65

6. 197 − 53

7. 116 + 239

8. 456 − 327

9. 272 + 351

10. 923 − 685

11. 49 + 327 + 22

12. 708 − 349

13. 203 + 75 + 81

14.
$$\begin{array}{r} 152 \\ + 398 \\ \hline \end{array}$$

15.
$$\begin{array}{r} 941 \\ - 621 \\ \hline \end{array}$$

16.
$$\begin{array}{r} 384 \\ - 139 \\ \hline \end{array}$$

17.
$$\begin{array}{r} 516 \\ 225 \\ + 394 \\ \hline \end{array}$$

Use with or after Lesson 4.1.

Write all of your answers on a separate sheet of paper.

For Problems 1–5, draw or build an array to help you solve each problem.

1. Tyler bought 3 boxes of snacks. Each box had 10 bags of snacks. How many bags of snacks did Tyler buy in all?

2. 4 pies are cut into 6 pieces each. How many pieces of pie are there in all?

3. Sharon bought 3 packs of invitations. Each pack had 8 invitations. How many invitations did Sharon buy in all?

4. Nancy displays her glass animals in a case with 5 shelves. Nancy puts 4 animals on each shelf. How many animals are in her display case?

5. Steve needs 5 inches of ribbon for each puppet that he is making. How many inches of ribbon will he need for 8 puppets?

For Problems 6–9, find the total value of each set of money.

6. 3 Q
2 D
4 P

7. 1 $1
2 Q
7 D
1 N

8. 2 $1
4 Q
3 D
4 N
3 P

9. 1 $1
5 Q
6 N
7 P

SRB
136–138

Find the area of each rectangle or square in square units. (Write your answers on a separate sheet of paper.)

10.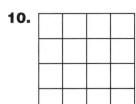

11.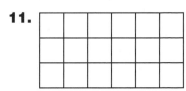

12.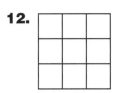

13.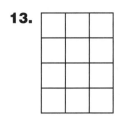

14.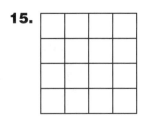

15.

Use with or after Lesson 4.2.

Write all of your answers on a separate sheet of paper.

For Problems 1–6, use counters or draw pictures to help you solve the division problems.

24 grapes shared equally ...

1. *by 3 people*   **2.** *by 4 people*   **3.** *by 6 people*

▨ grapes per person   ▨ grapes per person   ▨ grapes per person

▨ grapes left over   ▨ grapes left over   ▨ grapes left over

48 cherries shared equally ...

4. *by 6 people*   **5.** *by 8 people*   **6.** *by 12 people*

▨ cherries per person   ▨ cherries per person   ▨ cherries per person

▨ cherries left over   ▨ cherries left over   ▨ cherries left over

---

Subtract.

Unit
crackerjacks

7. $89 - 67$ **8.** $58 - 23$ **9.** $90 - 36$

10. $32 - 18$ **11.** $77 - 56$ **12.** $46 - 21$

13. $\begin{array}{r} 73 \\ -56 \\ \hline \end{array}$ **14.** $\begin{array}{r} 53 \\ -29 \\ \hline \end{array}$ **15.** $\begin{array}{r} 62 \\ -26 \\ \hline \end{array}$ **16.** $\begin{array}{r} 63 \\ -48 \\ \hline \end{array}$

Write all of your answers on a separate sheet of paper.

**For each problem, write a number model.
Then find the missing numbers.**

> **Example** 31 apples are divided evenly among 6 baskets.
> How many apples are in each basket?
>
> **Number model: 31 ÷ 6 → 5 R1**
>
> **6 apples are in each basket.
> 1 apple is left over.**

1. 24 bones are shared
equally among 6 dogs.
How many bones
does each dog get?

■ ÷ ■ → ■ R ■

Each dog gets ■ bones.
■ bones are left over.

2. Tim has 27 jars of jam.
He puts 4 jars in each
box. How many boxes
does he fill?

■ ÷ ■ → ■ R ■

Tim fills ■ boxes.
■ jars are left over.

Find the missing numbers.

3.

4,010　■　■　4,040　4,050　■　■

4.

3,712　3,812　■　■　4,112　■　■

5.

2,115　3,115　■　■　■　7,115

Find the missing numbers. (Write your answers on a separate sheet of paper.)

6.

in	out
12	8
14	10
	13
	15
	21

in ↓
| Rule |
| − 4 |
↓ out

7.

in	out
	15
	12
	20
	32
	40

in ↓
| Rule |
| + 8 |
↓ out

8.

in	out
	30
	27
	19
	16
	50

in ↓
| Rule |
| − 10 |
↓ out

9.

in	out
	8
	14
	20
	24
	50

in ↓
| Rule |
| Double |
↓ out

Write all of your answers on a separate sheet of paper.

Solve each multiplication problem. Then write a turn-around shortcut for each problem.

Example	$6 \times 2 = 12$	$2 \times 6 = 12$

1. 3×2 **2.** 4×3 **3.** 3×5

4. 6×3 **5.** 7×4 **6.** 2×4

Find each product.

7. 5×0 **8.** 7×1 **9.** 3×1

10. 16×1 **11.** 0×4 **12.** 12×0

Write each amount with dollars and cents.

Example	 $2.45

13. ⬚$1 Ⓠ Ⓠ Ⓓ Ⓓ Ⓟ Ⓟ Ⓟ

14. ⬚$1 ⬚$1 ⬚$1 Ⓠ Ⓓ Ⓓ Ⓝ Ⓟ Ⓟ

15. ⬚$10 ⬚$1 Ⓓ Ⓓ Ⓓ Ⓓ Ⓝ Ⓟ

16. ⬚$1 Ⓠ Ⓠ Ⓠ Ⓠ Ⓠ Ⓓ Ⓟ Ⓟ Ⓟ Ⓟ

**Find the missing number for each Fact Triangle.
Then write the family of facts for that triangle.**

Write all of your answers on a separate sheet of paper.

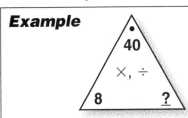

Example

Missing number: 5
Family of facts:
  8 × 5 = 40
  5 × 8 = 40
  40 ÷ 8 = 5
  40 ÷ 5 = 8

1.
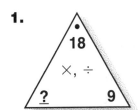

2.

3.
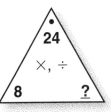

4.
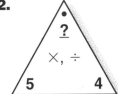

5.
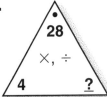

6.
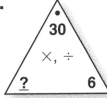

Write all of your answers on a separate sheet of paper.

Match each amount of money with an equal amount from the list at right. Then write the letter that identifies that amount.

7. fourteen dollars and two cents

8. $20.14

9. $41.20

10. $12.40

11. $10.42

12. twelve dollars and four cents

13. one dollar and forty-two cents

A. twelve dollars and forty cents

B. $12.04

C. forty-one dollars and twenty cents

D. $1.42

E. twenty dollars and fourteen cents

F. ten dollars and forty-two cents

G. $14.02

Find the missing numbers. You can use counters or draw pictures.

14. 15 pieces of candy
4 children share equally
■ pieces per child
■ pieces remaining

15. 12 tennis balls
3 balls per can
■ filled cans
■ balls remaining

16. 14 carrots
6 rabbits share equally
■ carrots per rabbit
■ carrots remaining

17. 27 books
8 books per box
■ filled boxes
■ books remaining

Copy each fact platter on a separate sheet of paper. Multiply the number in the *center* of the circle by each number *on* the circle. Then write the product *outside* the circle.

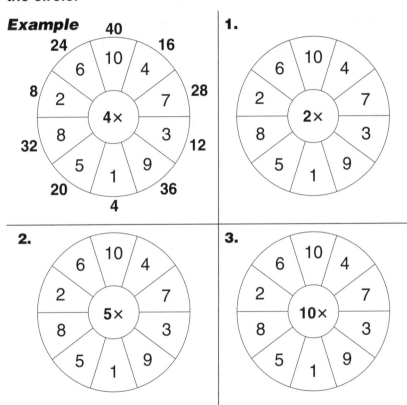

Example

40
24   16
6 10 4
8   2   28
  4×   7
32 8   3   12
  5   9
20 1   36
4

1.

10
6   4
2
2×   7
8   3
5   1   9

2.

10
6   4
2
5×   7
8   3
5   1   9

3.

10
6   4
2
10×   7
8   3
5   1   9

Tell what the underlined digit stands for in each number. (Write your answers on a separate sheet of paper.)

Example   5,416   5,000 or 5 thousands

4. 7<u>9</u>6   **5.** 7,51<u>4</u>   **6.** <u>6</u>48

7. 8,<u>9</u>54   **8.** <u>4</u>2,597   **9.** 9,0<u>4</u>6

10. 58,0<u>2</u>9   **11.** <u>6</u>,309   **12.** 3,1<u>8</u>9

SRB
63–66

Write a multiplication fact to find the total number of dots in each array.

Write all of your answers on a separate sheet of paper.

Example	• • • • • • •	$3 \times 7 = 21$
	• • • • • • •	21 total dots
	• • • • • • •	

13. • • • •
• • • •
• • • •
• • • •
• • • •

14. • • • •
• • • •
• • • •
• • • •
• • • •
• • • •

15. • •
• •
• •
• •
• •
• •

16. • • •
• • •
• • •
• • •
• • •
• • •
• • •

17. • • • • • • • •
• • • • • • • •
• • • • • • • •

18. • • • • •
• • • • •
• • • • •
• • • • •
• • • • •

Practice Set 28

Write all of your answers on a separate sheet of paper.

Answer each question using the numbers in the box.

| 79,512 | 29,517 | 12,759 | 27,951 | 95,721 |

1. Which numbers have 5 tens?

2. Which number has 5 thousands?

3. Which numbers have 1 ten?

4. Which numbers have 9 thousands?

5. Which number has 9 ten-thousands?

6. Which numbers have 7 hundreds?

7. Which number has 2 ones?

8. Which numbers have 5 hundreds?

9. Which numbers have 2 ten-thousands?

10. Which numbers have 1 one?

11. Which number has 7 thousands?

Find each product.

Unit
pink elephants

12. 1×7 **13.** 5×2

14. 8×2 **15.** 3×10

16. 6×5 **17.** 9×5

18. 10×5 **19.** 8×0 **20.** 6×1

Find the missing rule and the numbers for the empty frames.

Write all of your answers on a separate sheet of paper.

Example

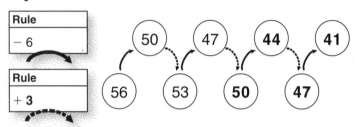

21.

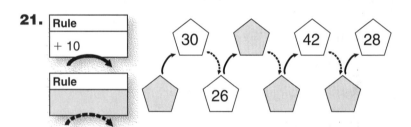

22.

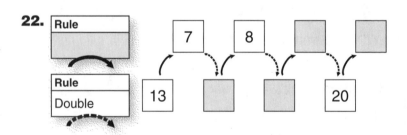

23.

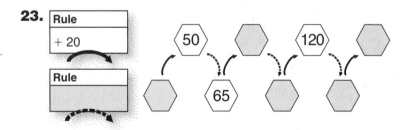

Write all of your answers on a separate sheet of paper.

Write each group of numbers in order from smallest to largest.

1. 4,289   4,892   2,489   9,842   4,982

2. 5,901   6,001   5,991   1,995   5,910   6,010

3. 10,453   1,543   11,246   21,101   9,878

4. 71,034   17,340   80,249   99,999   81,001

Use your calculator to count by 100s.
Find the missing numbers.

5. 2,300; 2,400; ■; ■; ■; 2,800; ■; ■; 3,100; 3,200

6. 7,260; 7,360; ■; ■; ■; 7,760; ■; ■; 8,060; ■

7. 5,408; 5,508; ■; ■; 5,808; 5,908; ■; ■; ■

8. 6,132; ■; ■; ■; 6,532; ■; ■; 6,832; ■; ■

9. 8,555; 8,655; ■; ■; ■; 9,055; ■; ■; ■; ■

Find the same time in the second list.
Write the letter that identifies that matching time.

10. 5 minutes after 3   **A.** 5:30

11. 10:40   **B.** half-past 7

12. quarter-to 5   **C.** 3:05

13. 7:30   **D.** 20 minutes to 11

14. five-thirty   **E.** 10:15

15. quarter-after 10   **F.** 4:45

Write all of your answers on a separate sheet of paper.

Write the following numbers using digits:

1. one million, two hundred twenty-eight thousand

2. six million, three thousand, four hundred

3. seven hundred thirty-one thousand,
five hundred forty-nine

4. eighty-three thousand, nine hundred two

5. four million, six hundred five

6. three million, twenty thousand, five hundred

**Add or subtract. Then make a ballpark estimate
to check that your answer makes sense.**

7. 721 − 350　　　**8.** 213 + 643　　　**9.** 672 − 514

10. 815 + 192　　**11.** 728 − 456　　**12.** 359 + 287

13.	821	**14.**	416	**15.**	89	**16.**	327
	− 371		− 203		+ 376		− 119

17.	223	**18.**	632	**19.**	551	**20.**	264
	+ 478		− 218		321		118
					+ 114		+ 319

Write all of your answers on a separate sheet of paper.

Write < or > for each ■.

> < means *is less than*
> > means *is greater than*

Example 59,423 ■ 59,389

Both numbers have 5 ten-thousands
and 9 thousands.

4 hundreds is greater than 3 hundreds.

Therefore: **59,423 > 59,389**

1. 127,675 ■ 137,675

2. 24,714 ■ 24,710

3. 159,338 ■ 160,273

4. 673,218 ■ 673,239

5. 285,641 ■ 385,641

6. 490,315 ■ 510,214

7. 331,846 ■ 330,259

8. 37,014 ■ 37,104

9. 999,972 ■ 999,992

10. 53,892 ■ 54,617

For each number below, write the number that is
10 more, 100 more, and 1,000 more.

Example 33,492
10 more: **33,502**
100 more: **33,592**
1,000 more: **34,492**

11. 52,416

12. 68,927

13. 72,499

14. 65,798

15. 95,281

16. 39,482

Write all of your answers on a separate sheet of paper.

Find each missing number.

> 1 meter = 10 decimeters
> 1 meter = 100 centimeters
> 1 decimeter = 10 centimeters

17. 3 meters = ■ decimeters

18. 300 centimeters = ■ meters

19. 70 centimeters = ■ decimeters

20. 8 meters = ■ decimeters

21. 4 decimeters = ■ centimeters

22. ■ centimeters = 5 meters

23. 400 centimeters = ■ meters

24. 20 decimeters = ■ meters

25. 100 decimeters = ■ meters

26. ■ decimeters = 100 centimeters

Find each answer.

27. 2×6

28. 1×18

29. 5×4

30. 7×3

31. 8×5

32. 6×5

33. $\begin{array}{r} 9 \\ \times\, 6 \\ \hline \end{array}$

34. $\begin{array}{r} 6 \\ \times\, 7 \\ \hline \end{array}$

35. $\begin{array}{r} 3 \\ \times\, 8 \\ \hline \end{array}$

36. $\begin{array}{r} 4 \\ \times\, 2 \\ \hline \end{array}$

37. $\begin{array}{r} 0 \\ \times\, 29 \\ \hline \end{array}$

38. $\begin{array}{r} 5 \\ \times\, 9 \\ \hline \end{array}$

39. $\begin{array}{r} 2 \\ \times\, 10 \\ \hline \end{array}$

40. $\begin{array}{r} 7 \\ \times\, 3 \\ \hline \end{array}$

Write a decimal for the shaded part of each grid.
Each grid is ONE.

Write your answers on a separate sheet of paper.

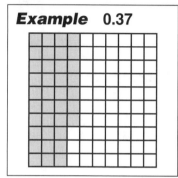

Example 0.37

1.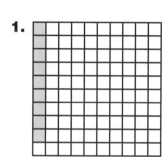

2.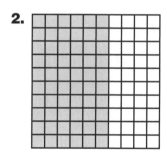

3.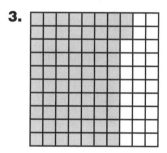

4.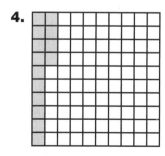

5.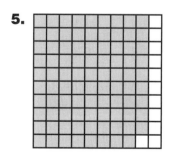

Practice Set 32 (cont.)

Write all of your answers on a separate sheet of paper.

Write each number using digits.

> **Example**   twenty-six thousand, four hundred twelve
> **26,412**

6. four thousand, six hundred ten

7. seventy-two thousand, eight hundred five

8. five thousand, six

9. sixty-seven thousand, three hundred eighteen

10. one hundred fourteen thousand,
five hundred thirty-six

11. seven hundred eighty thousand, two hundred

12. six hundred seventy-nine thousand, eight

13. four hundred three thousand, ninety-two

Use your calculator.
Write the answer in dollars and cents.

> **Example** $2.71 + 92¢ = **$3.63**

14. 67¢ + $1.21

15. $0.59 + 83¢ + 27¢

16. $3.41 + $1.08

17. 114¢ + 32¢

18. $0.65 + $0.84

19. $5.04 + 42¢ + 33¢

20. $0.84 + $2.86

21. 256¢ + $2.56

22. 49¢ + $1.92 + 67¢

23. $4.41 + $3.15 + $6.85

Use with or after Lesson 5.7.

Write all of your answers on a separate sheet of paper.

Use the decimals in the box to answer each question below.

| 0.03 | 0.34 | 0.45 | 0.56 | 0.67 | 0.78 | 0.89 |

1. Which number has 3 tenths?

2. Which number has 5 hundredths?

3. Which number has 7 tenths?

4. Which number has 9 hundredths?

5. Which number has 0 tenths?

6. Which number has 6 tenths and 7 hundredths?

7. Which number has 5 tenths and 6 hundredths?

8. Which number has 3 tenths and 4 hundredths?

Write the addition and subtraction fact family for each group of numbers.

Example   5, 6, 11
   $5 + 6 = 11$
   $6 + 5 = 11$
   $11 - 6 = 5$
   $11 - 5 = 6$

9. 2, 8, 10   **10.** 7, 8, 15   **11.** 9, 3, 12

12. 6, 7, 13   **13.** 9, 5, 14   **14.** 5, 4, 9

15. 3, 1, 4   **16.** 4, 6, 10   **17.** 6, 2, 8

Write all of your answers on a separate sheet of paper.

For each number below, write the number that is 10 less, 100 less, and 1,000 less.

Example   52,928
                10 less: 52,918
                100 less: 52,828
                1,000 less: 51,928

18. 27,386   **19.** 50,221   **20.** 38,482

21. 93,525   **22.** 27,058   **23.** 60,867

24. 62,505   **25.** 28,331   **26.** 83,471

Solve each problem. You can use counters or draw pictures.

27. David had 527 baseball cards in his collection. He got 85 more baseball cards for his birthday. How many baseball cards does he have now?

28. Jenny has 412 hockey cards and 843 basketball cards. How many more basketball cards than baseball cards does she have?

29. David has a book that holds 9 cards on each page. How many cards can he put in the book if the book has 10 pages? How many cards can he put in a book with 7 pages?

30. Jenny wants to give away 25 of her hockey cards to her three brothers. How many cards will each brother get if they share the cards equally? How many cards will be left over?

Use with or after Lesson 5.8.

Write all of your answers on a separate sheet of paper.

> = means *is equal to*
> < means *is less than*
> > means *is greater than*

Write <, >, or = for each ■.

1. 0.01 meter ■ 0.08 meter

2. 0.30 meter ■ 0.03 meter

3. 0.40 meter ■ 0.20 meter

4. 0.50 meter ■ 0.54 meter

5. 0.1 meter ■ 2 longs

6. 0.01 meter ■ 5 cubes

7. 0.07 meter ■ 7 cubes

8. 0.6 meter ■ 6 cubes

■ ← cube (1 cm)

▬▬▬ ← long (10 cm)

↖ meterstick

Write the multiplication and division fact family for each group of numbers.

Example   16, 8, 2

$$8 \times 2 = 16$$
$$2 \times 8 = 16$$
$$16 \div 2 = 8$$
$$16 \div 8 = 2$$

9. 4, 5, 20   **10.** 2, 4, 8   **11.** 3, 4, 12

12. 5, 2, 10   **13.** 9, 2, 18   **14.** 5, 6, 30

Write all of your answers on a separate sheet of paper.

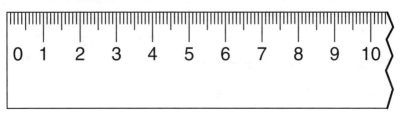

1. How many millimeters in a centimeter?

2. How many centimeters in a meter?

3. How many millimeters in 2 centimeters?

4. How many millimeters in a meter?

5. How many millimeters in 24.3 centimeters?

Estimate to answer *yes* or *no* to each question.

6. You have $9.00. Do you have enough to buy a book for $3.60, a magazine for $2.29, and a poster for $2.79?

7. You have $12.00. Do you have enough to buy a beach towel for $7.30 and sunglasses for $4.45?

8. You have $20.00. Do you have enough to buy a shirt for $11.40 and shorts for $7.39?

9. You have $15.00. Do you have enough to buy a fishing pole for $9.50, fishing line for $3.89, and bait for $1.79?

Write all of your answers on a separate sheet of paper.

Find each missing number.

1 m = 10 dm	1 dm = 0.1 m
1 m = 100 cm	1 cm = 0.01 m
1 dm = 10 cm	1 cm = 0.1 dm

10. ■ m = 400 cm   **11.** 0.8 dm = ■ cm

12. 60 cm = ■ dm   **13.** 0.5 m = ■ dm

14. ■ dm = 9 m   **15.** ■ cm = 0.02 m

16. 7 m = ■ cm   **17.** 0.4 m = ■ dm

18. 8 cm = ■ m   **19.** ■ m = 9 cm

20. ■ cm = 3 m   **21.** ■ cm = 0.9 dm

Find the missing numbers.

22.

420 ■ ■ ■ ■ 920 1,020 ■ ■ ■ 1,420

23.
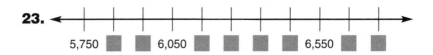
5,750 ■ ■ 6,050 ■ ■ ■ ■ 6,550 ■ ■

24.
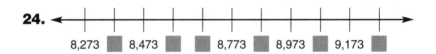
8,273 ■ 8,473 ■ ■ 8,773 ■ 8,973 ■ 9,173 ■

25.
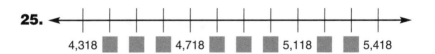
4,318 ■ ■ ■ 4,718 ■ ■ ■ 5,118 ■ ■ 5,418

Practice Set 36

Write all of your answers on a separate sheet of paper.

Match each number in the first list with the same number in the second list. Write the letter that identifies that matching number.

1. .5

2. two hundred one thousandths

3. .521

4. .05

5. 21 thousandths

6. 4 thousandths

7. .4

8. .2

9. 40 thousandths

10. .21

A. .004

B. 2 tenths

C. .040

D. 5 tenths

E. 21 hundredths

F. .201

G. 521 thousandths

H. .021

I. 4 tenths

J. 5 hundredths

Write < or > for each ■.

Unit
harbor seals

11. 465,243 ■ 564,243

12. 107,453 ■ 107,452

13. 999,999 ■ 1,000,000

14. 382,591 ■ 382,491

15. 848,484 ■ 484,848

16. 12,495 ■ 112,495

17. 359,416 ■ 369,416

18. 992,450 ■ 992,460

19. 600,770 ■ 600,707

20. 739,418 ■ 843,291

Use with or after Lesson 5.11.

Write all of your answers on a separate sheet of paper.

Count the number of line segments used to make each figure.

1.

2.

3.

4.

For each problem below, write a number model. Then find the missing numbers.

5. 12 pens are shared equally among 4 children. How many pens does each child get?

■ ÷ ■ → ■ R ■

Each child gets ■ pens.
■ pens are left over.

6. 8 toy mice are shared equally among 3 cats. How many mice does each cat get?

■ ÷ ■ → ■ R ■

Each cat gets ■ mice.
■ mice are left over.

7. Brian has 11 sweaters and puts 3 in each drawer. How many drawers does Brian fill?

■ ÷ ■ → ■ R ■

Brian fills ■ drawers.
■ sweaters are left over.

Practice Set 38

SRB 88–93

Write all of your answers on a separate sheet of paper.

Match each description with the correct example.
Write the letter that identifies that example.

1. parallel lines   **A.**

2. intersecting lines   **B.**

3. intersecting line segments   **C.**

4. parallel rays   **D.**

5. Draw a pair of parallel line segments.

6. Draw a pair of intersecting rays.

Write the multiplication and division fact family
for each group of numbers.

7. 25, 5, 5   **8.** 2, 4, 2

9. 8, 64, 8   **10.** 9, 9, 81

11. 42, 6, 7   **12.** 7, 7, 49

13. 8, 72, 9   **14.** 6, 30, 5

15. 27, 9, 3   **16.** 48, 6, 8

     Use with or after Lesson 6.2.

Measure each object to the nearest half-inch or half-centimeter.

Write your answers on a separate sheet of paper.

17.

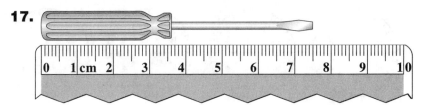

18.

19.

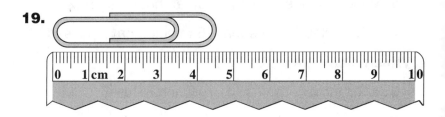

20.

21.

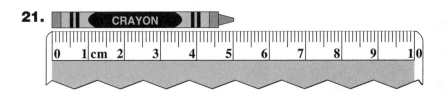

Write all of your answers on a separate sheet of paper.

The shaded part of each clock shows passing time.
Assume that each clock turns clockwise.

| A | B | C | D |

1. Which clock shows that one hour has passed?

2. Which clock shows that forty-five minutes have passed?

3. Which clock shows that half an hour has passed?

4. Which clock shows that 15 minutes have passed?

Which clock shows ...

5. a full turn?   **6.** a half-turn?

7. a quarter-turn?   **8.** a $\frac{3}{4}$ turn?

Draw an array to find each product.

9. 4×5 **10.** 3×8 **11.** 9×4

12. 2×7 **13.** 5×5 **14.** 6×1

15. 4×9 **16.** 7×4 **17.** 5×8

Use with or after Lesson 6.3.

Write all of your answers on a separate sheet of paper.

Find the area of each rectangle or square in square centimeters. Find the perimeter of each rectangle or square in centimeters.

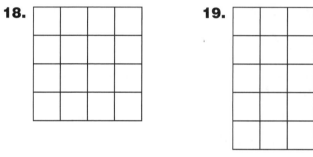

Example

Area: 12 square centimeters
Perimeter: 14 centimeters

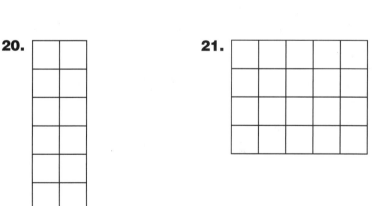

18.

19.

20.

21.

Write all of your answers on a separate sheet of paper.

1. Which shapes have right angles?

A.

B.

C.

D.

E.

Write the number that has ...

Example	4 tens	**30,947**
	9 hundreds	
	0 thousands	
	3 ten-thousands	
	7 ones	

2. 8 hundreds
9 ones
5 ten-thousands
3 tens
9 thousands

3. 4 thousands
6 tens
1 hundred
2 ones
7 ten-thousands

4. 7 hundreds
0 ones
3 ten-thousands
4 thousands
9 tens

5. 8 thousands
5 tens
2 hundreds
6 ten-thousands
8 ones

Match each description with the correct polygon.
Write the letter of that polygon. (Write your answers
on a separate sheet of paper.)

6. a rectangle with a perimeter of 22 in.

7. a triangle with a perimeter of 18 in.

8. a parallelogram with a perimeter of 18 in.

9. a square with a perimeter of 16 in.

10. a kite with a perimeter of 18 in.

11. a triangle with a perimeter of 17 in.

12. a rhombus with a perimeter of 28 in.

13. a rectangle with a perimeter of 20 in.

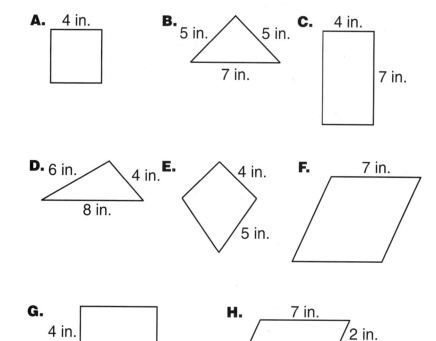

Write all of your answers on a separate sheet of paper.

Draw each angle as directed below. Record the direction of each turn with a curved arrow. And mark with a □ any right angle you make.

Example   Angle *H* shows a $\frac{3}{4}$ turn

1. An angle that shows a quarter-turn

2. An angle that shows a half-turn

3. An angle that shows a $\frac{3}{4}$ turn

4. An angle that is smaller than a half-turn

5. An angle that is larger than a half-turn

Draw an array to find each product.

	• • • • • • •	
Example 3 × 7	• • • • • • •	21
	• • • • • • •	

6. 2 × 5   **7.** 6 × 4   **8.** 1 × 8

9. 9 × 3   **10.** 5 × 6   **11.** 8 × 3

12. 5 × 1   **13.** 7 × 6   **14.** 5 × 9

Write all of your answers on a separate sheet of paper.

Each picture below shows one-half of a letter.
The dashed line is the line of symmetry.
Write the complete letter.

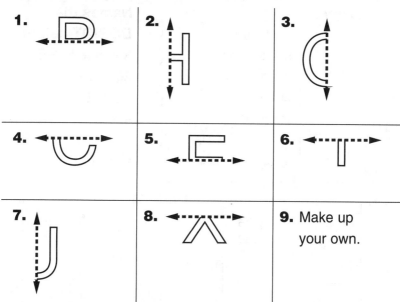

1.

2.

3.

4.

5.

6.

7.

8.

9. Make up your own.

Trace each shape below. Then draw the number of lines of symmetry shown in parentheses.

10. (3)

11. (2)

12. (1)

13. (1)

SRB 14 15

Write the names that DO NOT belong in each name-collection box. Then write the number that belongs on the label for each box. (Write your answers on a separate sheet of paper.)

Example

5 + 6 + 5 + 6
16 + 5   30 − 12
10 + 5 + 6
18 + 2
twenty-one
8 × 3   10 + 11

Names that DO NOT belong:

5 + 6 + 5 + 6
30 − 12
18 + 2
8 × 3

Label: 21

14.

4 × 8   15
3 × 10   7   + 15
× 4
20 + 13   ___
8 + 9 + 13
5 more than 25
5 × 6   3 × 9

15.

20 − 2   9
+ 9
• • • • • • • • •   ___
• • • • • • • • •
4 + 5 + 9   2 × 9
2 more than 15
₶₶₶ ₶₶₶ ₶₶₶ /   8
+ 9
4 less than 23   ___

16.

2 × 20   5
× 8
9 × 5   ___
6 less than 45
10 + 10 + 10 + 10
40 × 0   forty-one
14 + 26
5 more than 35

17.

20 less than 60   25
+ 25
14 + 36   10   ___
× 5
6 × 10   ___
20 + 20 + 10
0 × 50
30 + 25   100 − 5

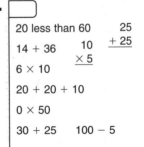

Write all of your answers on a separate sheet of paper.

Write the name of each solid. Tell how many faces, vertices, and edges each solid has.

Example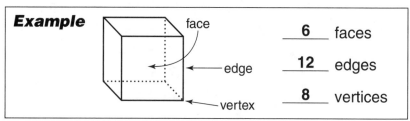

    face

    edge

    vertex

    ____6____ faces

    ___12___ edges

    ____8____ vertices

1.

2.

3.

4.

5.

Add.

Unit
marbles

6. 42 + 15   **7.** 31 + 29   **8.** 52 + 64

9. 37 + 61   **10.** 83 + 18   **11.** 34 + 68

12.   72
   + 87

13.   56
   + 25

14.   19
   + 31

15.   84
   + 4

Write all of your answers on a separate sheet of paper.

Write the multiplication and division fact family
for each Fact Triangle.

Example

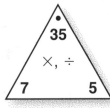

$7 \times 5 = 35$
$5 \times 7 = 35$
$35 \div 7 = 5$
$35 \div 5 = 7$

16.

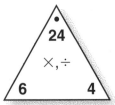

17.

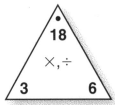

18.

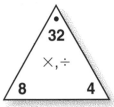

19.

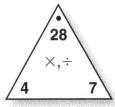

Write the multiplication and division fact family
for each group of numbers.

Example   5, 5, 25 $5 \times 5 = 25$
$25 \div 5 = 5$

20. 3, 3, 9   **21.** 16, 4, 4

22. 6, 36, 6   **23.** 49, 7, 7

24. 9, 81, 9   **25.** 8, 64, 8

Write all of your answers on a separate sheet of paper.

Sandy is making a design by pressing the bases of pyramids and prisms onto an ink pad. What shape can she make from each block?

> **Example**
>
>
>
> The base of a triangular prism makes a ___*triangle*___ .

1.

2.

3.

4.

5.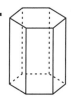

6.

Find the missing numbers. Count back by 1,000s.

7. 10,000; 9,000; ■; ■; ■; 5,000; ■; ■; ■; 1,000

8. 12,800; 11,800; ■; 9,800; ■; ■; ■; 5,800; ■; ■

9. 13,420; 12,420; ■; ■; ■; 8,420; ■; ■; ■; 4,420

10. 16,059; 15,059; ■; ■; ■; 11,059; ■; ■; ■; 7,059

11. 14,955; 13,955; ■; ■; ■; ■; 8,955; ■; ■; ■

Write all of your answers on a separate sheet of paper.

Write the number that has ...

Example	2 in the tenths place
	9 in the ones place
	6 in the tens place
	8 in the hundredths place **69.28**

12. 0 in the ones place
4 in the tenths place
8 in the tens place
9 in the hundredths place

13. 8 in the thousandths place
2 in the tenths place
6 in the ones place
5 in the hundredths place

14. 7 in the tenths place
0 in the hundredths place
9 in the tens place
4 in the ones place

15. 9 in the ones place
4 in the hundredths place
3 in the tenths place
8 in the thousandths place

16. 2 in the tens place
5 in the tenths place
9 in the ones place
6 in the hundredths place

17. 0 in the tenths place
4 in the thousandths place
7 in the hundredths place
2 in the ones place

Solve each problem. You can draw pictures or use counters.

18. Ginny bought 4 boxes of markers. Each box has 8 markers. How many markers did Ginny buy?

19. John has 18 roses. He puts 9 roses in each vase. How many vases does he fill? How many roses are left over?

20. Lia shared 22 cookies equally among 6 friends. How many cookies did each friend get? How many cookies were left over?

Practice Set 45

SRB
68
122 175

Write all of your answers on a separate sheet of paper.

Draw a square array for each square number. Then write the multiplication fact for each square number.

Example   25   • • • • •
                   • • • • •   5 × 5 = 25
                   • • • • •
                   • • • • •
                   • • • • •

1. 36	**2.** 16	**3.** 9
4. 4	**5.** 49	**6.** 64

Find the missing numbers.
You can use counters or draw pictures.

7. 26 crackers
6 children share equally
■ crackers per child
■ crackers left over

8. 36 pictures
9 pictures per page
■ filled pages
■ pages left over

9. 24 girls
4 girls per tent
■ filled tents
■ girls left over

10. 18 sheets of paper
4 children share equally
■ sheets per child
■ sheets left over

Find the corresponding letter on the centimeter ruler for each of the metric measures.

Example   2.5 centimeters is Point *A.*

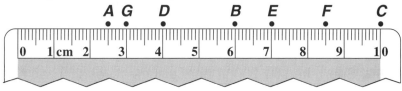

A G   D   B   E   F   C

11. 60 millimeters

12. 1 decimeter

13. 0.04 meter

14. 0.7 decimeter

15. 85 millimeters

16. 3 centimeters

Practice Set 45 (cont.)

SRB
18–21

Write all of your answers on a separate sheet of paper.

Write the number that is 10 more.

17. 14   **18.** 30   **19.** 539   **20.** 4,258   **21.** 7,904

Write the number that is 100 more.

22. 8   **23.** 27   **24.** 973   **25.** 2,918   **26.** 8,715

Write the number that is 1,000 more.

27. 7   **28.** 254   **29.** 5,791   **30.** 9,493   **31.** 12,463

Write the number that is 10 less.

32. 19   **33.** 142   **34.** 1,014   **35.** 7,420   **36.** 4,615

Write the number that is 100 less.

37. 156   **38.** 433   **39.** 5,212   **40.** 1,082   **41.** 12,617

Write the number that is 1,000 less.

42. 1,092   **43.** 7,214   **44.** 5,131   **45.** 10,673   **46.** 22,194

Find each answer using mental math.

47. 70 − 20   **48.** 400 + 500   **49.** 300 + 600 + 500

50. 800 − 600   **51.** 1,200 − 500   **52.** 4,000 + 9,000

53. 4,200 − 1,200   **54.** 6,300 + 800   **55.** 12,000 + 500

56. Sherri had $1,200 in her savings account. Then she took out $700. The next week she put $900 into her account. The following week, Sherri took out $300. How much is in her account now?

Use with or after Lesson 7.1.

Write the missing number for each Fact Triangle.
Then write the family of facts for that triangle. (Write
your answers on a separate sheet of paper.)

1.

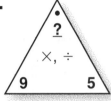

2.

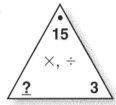

3.

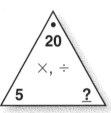

4.

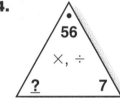

5.

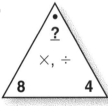

6.

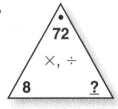

7.

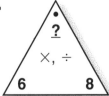

8.

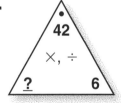

Write the missing rule and the missing numbers.
(Write your answers on a separate sheet of paper.)

Example

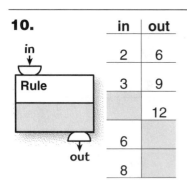

in	out
5	2
11	8
17	14
23	20
19	16

9.

in	out
4	16
10	22
	24
12	
20	

10.

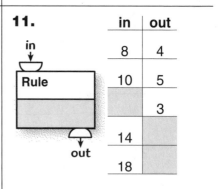

in	out
2	6
3	9
	12
6	
8	

11.

in	out
8	4
10	5
	3
14	
18	

Write all of your answers on a separate sheet of paper.

Solve.

1. 6 × 6   **2.** 8 × 3   **3.** 9 × 6   **4.** 9 × 9

5. 7 × 6   **6.** 8 × 8   **7.** 8 × 9   **8.** 8 × 4

9. 5 × 8   **10.** 9 × 4   **11.** 8 × 6   **12.** 7 × 7

13. 8 × 6   **14.** 7 × 8   **15.** 9 × 5   **16.** 7 × 9

Denise invented a game using this gameboard. Answer each question below.

17. How many rows are on Denise's gameboard? How many squares are in each row?

18. Write a number model to show the total number of squares on Denise's gameboard.

19. How many of the squares on the gameboard are black? How many are white?

20. If 2 markers can be placed on each square of the gameboard, how many markers can the gameboard hold?

Practice Set 48

SRB
16 17
182–185

Write all of your answers on a separate sheet of paper.

Write a number model. Then solve.

> **Example** Jerry picked **50** apples. He ate **2** of them. Then he divided the rest of the apples equally into **8** baskets. How many apples did he put in each basket?
>
> **Number model: (50 − 2) ÷ 8 = 6**

1. Karen made 3 clay pots Monday and 4 clay pots Tuesday. By the end of the week, she had made 17 pots. How many pots did she make between Wednesday and Friday?

2. Keneisha had 18 stickers. She put 2 of them on her notebook. She put 4 of them on each of her folders. How many folders did Keneisha have?

3. Franklin has 82 seashells. He wants to have 100. His friend Mario gave him 7. How many more shells does Franklin need?

4. Tim needs 24 cupcakes for his birthday party. His mother made 12. Tim has 4 friends who said they will bring the rest. How many cupcakes should each friend bring if all 4 friends bring equal amounts?

Find each answer.

5. For a picnic, Sharon brought 3 cookies for each of 4 people. How many cookies did she bring in all?

6. Tom bought 2 packages of postcards. Each package contained 5 postcards. How many postcards did he buy in all?

Use with or after Lesson 7.4.

Write all of your answers on a separate sheet of paper.

Write each number.

> **Example**
> one million, four hundred ten thousand, five hundred three
> **1,410,503**

7. three million, nine hundred fifty-four thousand,
six hundred twenty-nine

8. nine million, six hundred twenty-one thousand,
six hundred eight

9. two million, thirty-nine thousand,
four hundred ninety-eight

10. nine hundred forty-one thousand, eight hundred five

11. seven million, three thousand, two hundred eighty

12. six million, two hundred nine thousand,
four hundred fifty-five

13. nine million, eight hundred two

14. six million, nine thousand, ten

Write the multiplication and division fact family
for each group of numbers.

> **Example**   4, 28, 7 $4 \times 7 = 28$
> $7 \times 4 = 28$
> $28 \div 4 = 7$
> $28 \div 7 = 4$

15. 45, 9, 5   **16.** 32, 4, 8   **17.** 20, 4, 80

18. 6, 40, 240   **19.** 10, 6, 60   **20.** 30, 70, 210

Practice Set 49

SRB
64–66
182–185

Write all of your answers on a separate sheet of paper.

Answer each question.

1. How much are 7 [80s]?

2. How much are 4 [600s]?

3. How much are 2 [2,000s]?

4. How much are 3 [400s]?

5. Which number multiplied by 3 equals 90?

6. Which number multiplied by 4 equals 1,600?

7. Which number multiplied by 7 equals 490?

Solve each problem.

8. Sharon bought 3 packages of hair bows. There are 5 bows in each package. How many bows did Sharon buy?

9. Joe got 4 packages of stickers as a gift. Each package holds 6 stickers. How many stickers did Joe get?

10. A sheet of stamps has 6 rows. Each row has 3 stamps. How many stamps are on a sheet?

11. Each box of crackers holds 300 crackers. You have no boxes of crackers. How many crackers do you have?

12. Each row of buttons has 6 buttons. You have 1 row of buttons. How many buttons do you have?

13. 5 cakes are each cut into 6 pieces. How many pieces of cake are there?

Use with or after Lesson 7.6.

Write all of your answers on a separate sheet of paper.

Measure each line segment to the nearest centimeter. Then tell whether the line segments are *parallel* or *intersecting*.

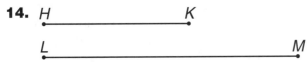

Example

Line segment *AB* is 3 cm long.
Line segment *CD* is 5 cm long.
These line segments are intersecting.

14.

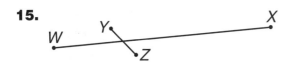

15.

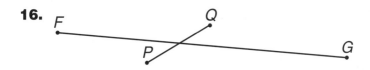

16.

Trace and finish each symmetrical shape according to the line of symmetry.

Example

17.

18.

Practice Set 50

Write all of your answers on a separate sheet of paper.

Use estimation to solve each of these problems:

1. Laura has $45.00. Does she have enough to buy 2 skirts that each cost $14.50 and a blouse that costs $17.00?

2. Dennis has $80.00. Does he have enough to buy gifts for his family that cost $23.50, $18.90, $15.95, and $17.50?

3. Linda earned $33.00 in January and $22.00 in February. She paid her sister back $9.00 that she owed her. Does Linda have enough money left to pay for a weekend trip that costs $48.00?

4. Dave earned $24.00 in July by cutting lawns. He earned $29.00 in August and $17.00 in September. Did Dave earn enough money to buy 2 games that cost $33.99 each?

5. Jill, JoAnn, and Jackie want go to an amusement park. The admission fee for each girl will be $22.95. Lunch for each girl will cost $5.50. Each girl received $30.00 for her birthday. Do they have enough money to go to the amusement park?

Find each missing number.

6. $4 = 2 \times \blacksquare$

7. $\blacksquare = 8 \times 0$

8. $\blacksquare \times 5 = 25$

9. $8 \div 1 = \blacksquare$

10. $4 \times \blacksquare = 4$

11. $0 = \blacksquare \times 0$

12. $9 = \blacksquare \div 1$

13. $\blacksquare = 3 \times 6$

14. $27 = \blacksquare \times 9$

15. $4 \times 7 = \blacksquare$

16. $3 \times \blacksquare = 12$

17. $\blacksquare \times 10 = 30$

18. $\blacksquare = 50 \times 1$

19. $1 \div \blacksquare = 1$

20. $\blacksquare \times 6 = 18$

Use with or after Lesson 7.7.

Write all of your answers on a separate sheet of paper.

Multiply.

1. 7 × 90   **2.** 40 × 40   **3.** 10 × 280   **4.** 5 × 50

5. 70 × 6   **6.** 400 × 8   **7.** 69 × 10   **8.** 28 × 10

9. 100 × 30   **10.** 70 × 30   **11.** 500 × 2   **12.** 8 × 300

Draw the following figures:

13. 2 parallel lines

14. 2 intersecting line segments

15. a right angle

16. 2 rays that form an angle

17. an angle that is smaller than a right angle

18. an angle that shows a half-turn

Find the median for each set of numbers below.

Example	12 16 7 18 13 10
Step 1	Put the numbers in order from least to greatest: 7 10 12 13 16 18
Step 2	Now find the middle value, or the value that has an equal number of values less than and greater than itself.
	The median, or middle value, is between 12 and 13.

19. 27 50 42 18 42   **20.** 36 9 17 24 28 15 14

21. 82 75 79 81   **22.** 15 30 19 28 34 11

23. 62 28 55 49 38   **24.** 83 34 68 58 68 97

Write all of your answers on a separate sheet of paper.

Show each amount of money using the fewest coins and bills possible. Use $1 **s,** Q **s,** D **s,** N **s, and** P **s.**

Example $1.86	$1 Q Q Q D P

25. 79¢   **26.** $0.93   **27.** $1.52

28. 49¢   **29.** $0.65   **30.** $2.19

31. $0.98   **32.** $3.84   **33.** 59¢

Solve each problem. Then make a ballpark estimate to check that your answer makes sense.

34. Dave caught a fish that was 26 inches long. Kim caught a fish that was 42 inches long. How much longer was Kim's fish?

35. The lowest temperature in Denver one year was 8°F. The highest temperature during that same year was 96°F. What was the difference between the two temperatures?

36. In the morning, the temperature was 24°F. By 2:00 in the afternoon, the temperature was 47°F. How much had the temperature risen?

37. Larry planted a bush that was 38 centimeters tall. Three months later the bush was 51 centimeters tall. How much had the bush grown?

Practice Set 52

Write all of your answers on a separate sheet of paper.

Use the following information to answer the questions below:

A school cafeteria can spend $1.50 on each student per lunch. One hamburger costs the school $1.50. One hot dog, however, costs the school only $0.50.

1. How many hot dogs can replace 1 hamburger?

2. How many hot dogs can replace 2 hamburgers?

3. How many hot dogs can replace 50 hamburgers?

4. How many hot dogs can replace 400 hamburgers?

Write the number that has ...

5. 1 hundred-thousand
4 tens
5 ten-thousands
7 ones
9 thousands
3 hundreds

6. 7 ten-thousands
2 ones
9 hundreds
0 thousands
3 hundred-thousands
9 tens

7. 4 hundreds
8 ones
5 hundred-thousands
2 tens
9 thousands
0 ten-thousands

8. 6 thousands
7 ten-thousands
6 ones
8 hundreds
4 tens
5 hundred-thousands

Match each description with the correct square or rectangle below. Write the letter that identifies the square or rectangle. (Write your answers on a separate sheet of paper.)

9. a rectangle with a perimeter of 18 units

10. a square with an area of 25 square units

11. a rectangle with an area of 10 square units

12. a rectangle with a perimeter of 10 units

13. a square with a perimeter of 20 units

14. a square that has the same number for its perimeter and its area

15. a rectangle that has an area of 14 square units

16. a rectangle that has a perimeter of 14 units

A.

B.

C.

D.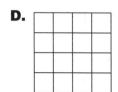

E.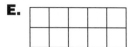

F.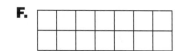

Write the fraction for the shaded part of each picture.
(Write your answers on a separate sheet of paper.)

Example

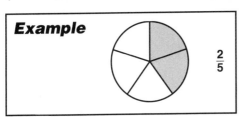

$\frac{2}{5}$

1.

2.

3.

4.

5.

6

7.

8.

Write all of your answers on a separate sheet of paper.

Find the missing numbers on each number line.

1.

2.

3.

4.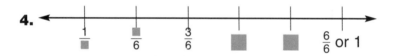

5.

Find each missing number.
You can use the number lines above to help you.

> **Example** $1 = \frac{6}{\blacksquare}$ $1 = \frac{6}{6}$

6. $\frac{1}{2} = \frac{\blacksquare}{8}$ **7.** $\frac{4}{4} = \frac{\blacksquare}{3}$

8. $\frac{\blacksquare}{6} = \frac{2}{3}$ **9** $\frac{\blacksquare}{8} = 1$

10. $\frac{6}{8} = \frac{\blacksquare}{4}$ **11.** $\frac{1}{\blacksquare} = \frac{2}{6}$

12. $\frac{3}{3} = \frac{8}{\blacksquare}$ **13.** $\frac{\blacksquare}{8} = \frac{1}{4}$

14. $\frac{\blacksquare}{2} = \frac{3}{\blacksquare} = \frac{4}{8} = \frac{\blacksquare}{4}$

Write as many numbers as you can for the fractional parts shown in each picture. (Write your answers on a separate sheet of paper.)

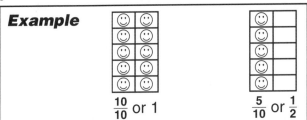

Example

$\frac{10}{10}$ or 1

$\frac{5}{10}$ or $\frac{1}{2}$

1.

2.

$\frac{8}{8}$ or 1

3.

4.

$\frac{6}{6}$ or 1

5.

6.

$\frac{5}{5}$ or 1

7.

8.

$\frac{4}{4}$ or 1

Write all of your answers on a separate sheet of paper.

Measure each object to the nearest half-inch.

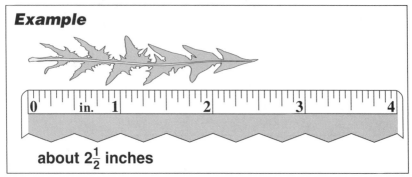

Example

about $2\frac{1}{2}$ inches

9.

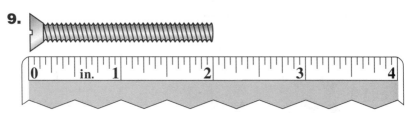

10.

11.

Find each product.

12. 1×8 **13.** 0×5 **14.** 15×1

15. 24×0 **16.** 1×37 **17.** 145×0

Write >, < or = for each ■. (Write your answers on a separate sheet of paper.)

Example This is ONE: $\frac{3}{6}$ ■ $\frac{2}{6}$

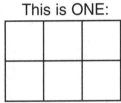

< means *is less than*

> means *is greater than*

$\frac{3}{6}$ > $\frac{2}{6}$

---

1. This is ONE:

$\frac{1}{2}$ ■ $\frac{2}{4}$ $\frac{3}{4}$ ■ $\frac{1}{4}$

2. This is ONE:

$\frac{5}{8}$ ■ $\frac{3}{4}$ $\frac{1}{2}$ ■ $\frac{4}{8}$

3. This is ONE:

$\frac{1}{2}$ ■ $\frac{3}{6}$ $\frac{1}{3}$ ■ $\frac{1}{6}$

4. This is ONE:

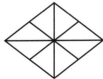

$\frac{3}{8}$ ■ $\frac{1}{4}$ $\frac{2}{8}$ ■ $\frac{1}{4}$

Write the missing numbers in the tables. Write your answers on a separate sheet of paper.

5.

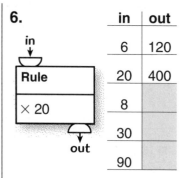

in	out
17	117
106	206
314	
1,462	
5,067	

6.

in
Rule
× 20
out

in	out
6	120
20	400
8	
30	
90	

7.

in
Rule
× 0
out

in	out
5	0
19	
108	
2,416	
9,999	

8.

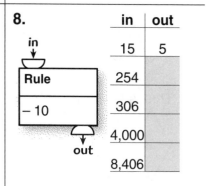

in	out
15	5
254	
306	
4,000	
8,406	

Write all of your answers on a separate sheet of paper.

Write both a fraction and a mixed number
to match each picture.

1.

2.

3.

Find the missing number for each Fact Triangle.
Then write the fact family for that triangle.

4.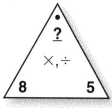

5.

6.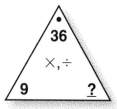

7.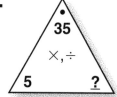

Practice Set 57 (cont.)

Write all of your answers on a separate sheet of paper.

Complete the number models.

8. $(4 \times 3) + 12 =$ ■   **9.** $40 = (24 + 36) -$ ■

Use the numbers in each addition sentence below
to write another addition sentence
and two subtraction sentences.

Example   19 + 6 = 25
6 + 19 = 25
25 − 6 = 19
25 − 19 = 6

10. $8 + 6 = 14$ **11.** $5 + 9 = 14$

12. $7 + 34 = 41$ **13.** $10 + 7 = 17$

14. $56 + 8 = 64$ **15.** $40 + 30 = 70$

16. $100 + 4 = 104$ **17.** $93 + 6 = 99$

18. $200 + 500 = 700$ **19.** $400 + 600 = 1,000$

Find an equal amount of money in the second list.
Write the letter that identifies that amount.

20. $\frac{1}{100}$ dollar   **A.** $0.05

21. $\frac{1}{5}$ quarter   **B.** $\frac{1}{10}$ dollar

22. quarter   **C.** penny

23. $\frac{1}{2}$ dollar   **D.** 25¢

24. 10¢   **E.** 50¢

25. $0.75   **F.** $\frac{3}{4}$ dollar

Practice Set 58

Write all of your answers on a separate sheet of paper.

Solve each problem.

1. Sharon brought 12 apples to the picnic. After the picnic, 2 apples were left. What fraction of the apples were eaten?

2. Dave spent 5 days at camp. What fraction of a week did Dave spend at camp?

3. Dorothy bought 10 yards of ribbon. She used 2 yards to wrap packages. What fraction of the ribbon did she use?

4. Glenda had $15. She spent $9 on a book. What fraction of her money did Glenda spend on the book?

5. For a party, a huge sandwich was cut into 25 pieces. After the party, 5 pieces were left. What fraction of the sandwich was eaten? What fraction of the sandwich was not eaten?

6. A vase of flowers has 6 red roses, 6 yellow roses, and 12 white roses. What fraction of the roses are yellow? What fraction of the flowers are white?

Make your own name-collection box for each number. Include +, −, ×, and ÷ at least once in each box. Include at least 8 different names for each number.

Example

45
15 + 15 + 15
0 + 45   37 + 8
9 × 5   55 − 10
45 ÷ 1   60 − 15
4 tens and 5 ones

7. 30

8. 25

9. 40

10. 28

11. 60

Write all of your answers on a separate sheet of paper.

Solve each problem.

1. a. 200 [400s]   **b.** 200 × 400

2. a. 300 [500s]   **b.** 300 × 500

3. How many 500s are in 2,000?

4. How many 300s are in 3,000?

5. How many 200s are in 2,000?

Solve each problem. Circle the square products.

6. 7 × 4   **7.** 4 × 4   **8.** 6 × 6

9. 9 × 9   **10.** 8 × 8   **11.** 7 × 8

12. 6 × 9   **13.** 7 × 7   **14.** 9 × 8

15. 5 × 5   **16.** 8 × 6   **17.** 7 × 9

Write a mixed number for each fraction.
Draw pictures to help you.

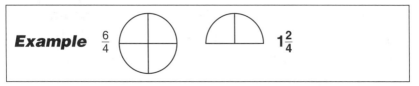

Example $\frac{6}{4}$ $1\frac{2}{4}$

18. $\frac{3}{2}$ **19.** $\frac{6}{5}$ **20.** $\frac{7}{3}$

Write all of your answers on a separate sheet of paper.

Solve the following problems mentally:

Carton   Tray

1. How many eggs are in 2 cartons?

2. How many eggs are in 1 tray?

3. How many eggs are in half a tray?

4. How many eggs are in 3 cartons?

5. How many eggs in half a carton?

6. Which is more, 4 cartons or 1 tray?

Find each missing number.

Example	2 gloves
	double 2 gloves = **4 gloves**
	triple 2 gloves = **6 gloves**
	quadruple 2 gloves = **8 gloves**
	5 times 2 gloves = **10 gloves**
	10 times 2 gloves = **20 gloves**

7. 3¢

double 3¢ = ■ ¢
triple 3¢ = ■ ¢
quadruple 3¢ = ■ ¢
5 times 3¢ = ■ ¢
10 times 3¢ = ■ ¢

8. 4 inches

double 4 in. = ■ in.
triple 4 in. = ■ in.
quadruple 4 in. = ■ in.
5 times 4 in. = ■ in.
10 times 4 in. = ■ in.

Write the fraction for the shaded part of the picture in two different ways. (Write your answers on a separate sheet of paper.)

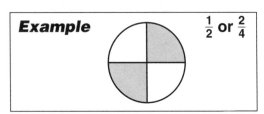

Example $\frac{1}{2}$ or $\frac{2}{4}$

9.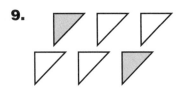

10.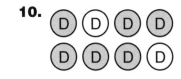

11.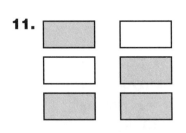

12.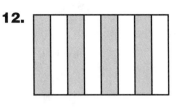

13.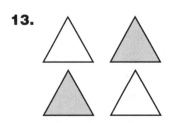

14.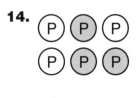

Use with or after Lesson 9.2.

Practice Set 61

Write all of your answers on a separate sheet of paper.

Multiply. Then *check* your answers using a calculator.

Example 29
× 3
3 [20s]   60
3 [9s]   27
60 + 27   **87**

1. 51
  × 6

2. 84
  × 5

3. 17
  × 8

4. 206
  × 9

5. 419
  × 4

**For each problem below, write a number model.
Then find the missing numbers.**

6. Donna puts 6 pears in each bag. She has 32 pears.
How many bags does she fill?

   ■ ÷ ■ → ■ R ■

   Donna fills ■ bags.

   ■ pears are left over.

7. 21 signs are shared equally by 4 classrooms.
How many signs does each classroom get?

   ■ ÷ ■ → ■ R ■

   Each classroom gets ■ signs.

   ■ signs are left over.

Write all of your answers on a separate sheet of paper.

Solve each number story using the grocery store sign.

— Special —	
Peaches	$0.50 each
Apples	$0.39 each
Pears	$0.61 each
(No tax)	

1. Sandra has $2.00. Can she buy 5 apples?
How much money will she have left?

2. How much money does Kenny need to buy 4 pears?

3. How much does it cost to buy 6 pears and 3 apples?

Multiply. Circle each square product.

4. 7 × 9	**5.** 8 × 8	**6.** 6 × 7
7. 4 × 8	**8.** 5 × 5	**9.** 9 × 9
10. 6 × 6	**11.** 7 × 7	**12.** 8 × 9
13. 8 × 7	**14.** 6 × 8	**15.** 6 × 6

Change each mixed number to a fraction.
Draw pictures to help you.

Example $1\frac{2}{3}$ ⬤ ⬤ $\frac{5}{3}$

16. $2\frac{1}{2}$ **17.** $3\frac{3}{4}$ **18.** $1\frac{3}{6}$

Solve each problem. (Write your answers on a separate sheet of paper.)

19. Each red fox weighs 19 pounds. How much do 7 red foxes weigh?

20. Ben spent 25 minutes walking to school. What fraction of an hour is this? (*Hint:* 1 hour = 60 minutes.)

21. Betty has 25 stickers. She wants to share them equally among 3 friends. How many stickers will each friend get? How many stickers will be left over?

22. Ellen had $30.00. She spent $14.00 shopping. What fraction of her money did she spend? What fraction of her money did she NOT spend?

23. Sam's birthday cake was cut into 16 pieces. After his party, 3 pieces were left. What fraction of his cake was left? What fraction of his cake was eaten?

24. Ruth wants to buy 4 computer games that each cost $29.50. About how much money does Ruth need in order to buy all 4 computer games?

25. Jan wants to get her hair cut and buy shampoo. Jan has $25.00. Does she have enough money for a haircut that costs $16.00 and 2 bottles of shampoo that cost $4.25 each?

26. A quilt has 5 yellow squares, 10 blue squares, and 10 green squares. What fraction of the squares are blue? What fraction of the squares are yellow? What fraction of the squares are red?

Practice Set 63

Write all of your answers on a separate sheet of paper.

Read the information below.
Then answer each question.

Ted has 36 flowers. He wants to put the flowers into vases. He wants each vase to have the same number of flowers—without any flowers being left over.

1. Can he put the flowers in 1 vase? 2 vases? 3 vases? If so, how many flowers go in each vase?

2. Can he put the flowers in 4 vases? 5 vases? 6 vases? If so, how many flowers go in each vase?

3. Can he put the flowers in 7 vases? 8 vases? 9 vases? If so, how many flowers go in each vase?

4. Can he put the flowers in 10 vases? 11 vases? 12 vases? If so, how many flowers go in each vase?

> *The factors of 36* are the numbers that can be multiplied by whole numbers to get 36 or the numbers that 36 can be divided by without having remainders.

5. Name the factors of 36.

For each number below, give the value of each digit.

Example 48.613	The 4 means 4 tens.
	The 8 means 8 ones.
	The 6 means 6 tenths.
	The 1 means 1 hundredth.
	The 3 means 3 thousandths.

6. 295.6   **7.** 30.48   **8.** 10.925

Use with or after Lesson 9.6.

Write the number family for each Fact Triangle.
(Write your answers on a separate sheet of paper.)

Example

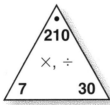

$7 \times 30 = 210$

$30 \times 7 = 210$

$210 \div 7 = 30$

$210 \div 30 = 7$

9.

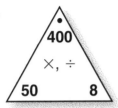

10.

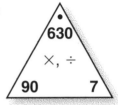

11.

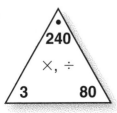

12.

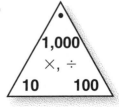

13.

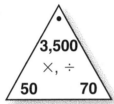

14.

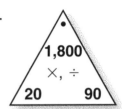

Write all of your answers on a separate sheet of paper.

Solve each problem.

1. $56 ÷ 8   **2.** $81 ÷ 9   **3.** $54 ÷ 6

4. $150 ÷ 6   **5.** $120 ÷ 8   **6.** $140 ÷ 7

7. $122 ÷ 4   **8.** $85 ÷ 5   **9.** $490 ÷ 7

Find the missing numbers. Use fractions.

10.

11.

12.

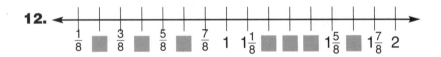

13.

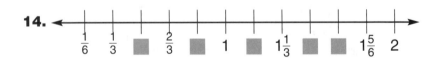

14.

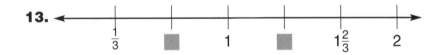

Write all of your answers on a separate sheet of paper.

Solve each problem.

1. Ken wants to put 6 ounces of water in each glass. How many glasses can he fill with 42 ounces of water? How many ounces of water will be left over?

2. Lynn wants to cut a 50-inch piece of string into pieces that are each 8 inches long. How many 8-inch pieces can she cut? How many inches of string will be left over?

Write the number that has ...

3. 7 in the tens place
1 in the thousands place
4 in the tenths place
2 in the hundreds place
6 in the ones place

4. 4 in the hundredths place
1 in the tens place
5 in the ones place
7 in the tenths place
9 in the hundreds place

5. 0 in the tenths place
9 in the thousandths place
2 in the ones place
5 in the tens place
8 in the hundredths place

6. 0 in the hundredths place
6 in the ones place
1 in the tens place
9 in the thousandths place
3 in the tenths place

7. 3 in the hundreds place
9 in the ones place
8 in the tenths place
4 in the tens place
6 in the thousands place
7 in the hundredths place

8. 4 in the tenths place
2 in the thousands place
0 in the tens place
6 in the thousandths place
1 in the ones place
0 in the hundredths place
4 in the hundreds place

Practice Set 66

Write all of your answers on a separate sheet of paper.

Use lattice multiplication to solve each problem.

1. 8 × 49 **2.** 7 × 359 **3.** 6 × 314

4. 9 × 68 **5.** 5 × 456 **6.** 7 × 834

Write a multiplication fact to find the area of each square.

Example		3 × 3 = 9 Area = 9 square units

7.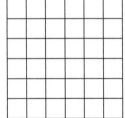

8.

9.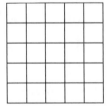

10.

Write all of your answers on a separate sheet of paper.

Multiply using the partial-products method.
Then use a calculator to check each answer.

Example	78
	× 43
(40 × 70)	2,800
(40 × 8)	320
(3 × 70)	210
(3 × 8)	24
	3,354

1. 29
× 14

2. 34
× 51

3. 62
× 22

4. 44
× 36

5. 81
× 53

6. 39
× 28

7. 76
× 64

Use estimation to solve each problem.

8. Dina has $25.00. Does she have enough to buy a radio that costs $14.79 and a CD that costs $11.25?

9. Jaime has $40.00. Does he have enough to buy shoes that cost $21.97 and two ties that cost $8.50 each?

10. Janice has $50.00. How many plants can she buy if each plant costs $11.95?

11. Jack has $60.00. How many shirts can he buy if each shirt costs $14.50?

12. Jason has $63.00 in his savings account. He received $35.00 as birthday gifts. Does he have enough money to buy a bike that costs $90.00?

Write all of your answers on a separate sheet of paper.

Solve each problem.

13. Arthur bought a goldfish for 49¢, a striped fish for $0.72, and fish food for 68¢. How much did Arthur spend?

14. How much change did Arthur receive if he paid for the 3 items with $3.00?

15. Betty wants to buy a dog collar for $3.50, a water dish for $2.79, and a toy bone for $3.49. Can she buy all 3 items with $10.00?

16. How much do the 3 items that Betty wants to buy cost altogether?

Write >, <, or = for each ■.

17. This is ONE:

$\frac{2}{4}$ ■ $\frac{1}{4}$ $\frac{3}{4}$ ■ $\frac{1}{2}$

18. This is ONE:

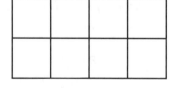

$\frac{5}{8}$ ■ $\frac{1}{2}$ $\frac{1}{4}$ ■ $\frac{2}{8}$

19. This is ONE:

$\frac{2}{3}$ ■ $\frac{4}{6}$ $\frac{1}{3}$ ■ $\frac{1}{2}$

Write all of your answers on a separate sheet of paper.

**Write the number and the unit for each problem.
Use Celsius temperatures.**

> **Example** 4 degrees below zero −4°C

1. 25 degrees above zero

2. 58 degrees below zero

3. zero degrees

4. 150 degrees above zero

5. 14 degrees below zero

6. 100 degrees below zero

**Which temperature is colder? You
can use the thermometer to help you.**

> **Example** −6°C or −14°C
> −14°C is below −6°C on
> the thermometer.
> **−14°C is colder than −6°C.**

7. 0°C or 5°C   **8.** 2°C or −20°C

9. 9°C or −9°C   **10.** −7°C or 0°C

**Which temperature is warmer? You
can use the thermometer to help you.**

> **Example** 24°C or −2°C
> 24°C is above −2°C on
> the thermometer.
> **24°C is warmer than −2°C.**

11. 0°C or −8°C   **12.** −98°C or 1°C

13. 15°C or −15°C **14.** 12°C or −35°C

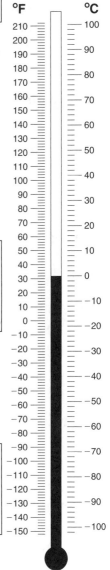

Write all of your answers on a separate sheet of paper.

Complete the list of factors for each number below.

> *The factors of a number* are the numbers that
> can be multiplied by whole numbers to get that
> number or the numbers that a number can be
> divided by without having remainders.

Example   Factors of 16: 1, ■, ■, 8, ■

             Factors of 16: 1, 2, 4, 8, 16

15. Factors of 7: ■, 7

16. Factors of 18: ■, 2, ■, ■, ■, 18

17. Factors of 36: 1, ■, ■, 4, ■, 9, ■, ■, 36

18. Factors of 50: ■, 2, ■, ■, 25, ■

Solve each problem.

19. Jerry went swimming 19 days in June. What fraction of the days in June did Jerry go swimming? (*Hint:* June has 30 days.)

20. Sarah spent 20 minutes eating breakfast. What fraction of an hour did she spend eating breakfast? What fraction of an hour did she NOT spend eating breakfast?

21. Sam and two friends shared a pizza cut into 8 pieces. Sam ate 1 piece, and each of his friends ate 2 pieces. What fraction of the pizza did Sam eat? What fraction of the pizza did each friend eat? What fraction of the pizza was left over?

SRB
182–195
270

Write all of your answers on a separate sheet of paper.

Find each missing number. Use fractions.

> 1 meter = 10 decimeters   1 yard = 3 feet
> 1 meter = 100 centimeters 1 yard = 36 inches
> 1 decimeter = 10 centimeters   1 foot = 12 inches
> 1 centimeter = 10 millimeters

1. ■ yard = 12 inches   **2.** ■ meter = 8 decimeters

3. 1 foot = ■ yard   **4.** 50 centimeters = ■ meter

5. 9 inches = ■ foot   **6.** ■ centimeter =
3 millimeters

7. ■ yard = 2 feet   **8.** 9 centimeters = ■ meter

9. ■ meter =
2 decimeters   **10.** ■ decimeter =
3 centimeters

11. 5 inches = ■ foot   **12.** ■ meter = 3 centimeters

**Find each answer. You can draw pictures
or use counters.**

13. There are 12 students
taking swimming lessons.
$\frac{1}{3}$ of them are third
graders. How many
are third graders?

14. The pet store has
10 dogs for sale. Half
of the dogs are collies.
How many of the dogs
are collies?

15. Karen drew a picture of 8 flags. She colored $\frac{1}{4}$ of the
flags orange. How many flags did she color orange?
What fraction of the flags did she NOT color orange?

For each ruler, find the distance between the two points. (Write your answers on a separate sheet of paper.)

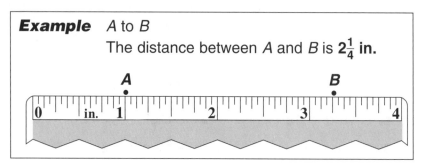

Example   *A* to *B*
The distance between *A* and *B* is $2\frac{1}{4}$ in.

A   **B**

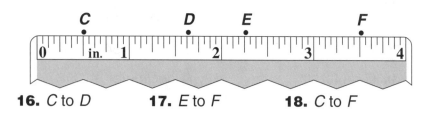

C   **D**   **E**   **F**

16. *C* to *D*   **17.** *E* to *F*   **18.** *C* to *F*

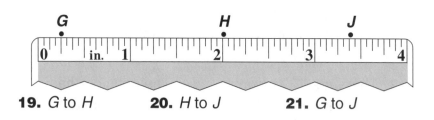

G   **H**   **J**

19. *G* to *H*   **20.** *H* to *J*   **21.** *G* to *J*

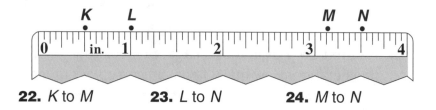

K   **L**   **M** **N**

22. *K* to *M*   **23.** *L* to *N*   **24.** *M* to *N*

Practice Set 70

Write all of your answers on a separate sheet of paper.

Find the volume of each box.
Each cube stands for 1 cubic centimeter.

1.

2.

3.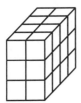

4.

Tell which unit you would use to measure each item.
Choose from inch, foot, yard, and mile.

> **Example**   the length of a pencil
> **Unit: inch**

5. the length of your math book

6. the length of a paper clip

7. the distance between Chicago and St. Louis

8. the length of a football field

9. the width of your hand

10. the width of a room

11. the width of your foot

12. the width of a park

13. the distance traveled in a car after one hour

14. the height of a dog

Write all of your answers on a separate sheet of paper.

Which temperature is colder? You
can use the thermometer to help you.

15. 0°F or –18°F   **16.** 12°F or –12°F

17. 0°F or 6°F   **18.** –8°F or –18°F

19. 5°F or 15°F   **20.** –23°F or –32°F

Which temperature is warmer? You
can use the thermometer to help you.

21. 6°C or 36°C   **22.** –14°C or –45°C

23. 0°C or –10° C   **24.** 12°C or –12°C

25. 16°C or –37°C   **26.** 20°C or 0°C

Solve each problem. You can
use the thermometer to help you.

27. One January morning, the
temperature was –18°F. By noon,
the temperature had risen to 4°F.
How many degrees had the
temperature risen?

28. One June morning, the temperature
was 18°C. By 2:00 in the afternoon,
the temperature had risen to 34°C.
How many degrees had the
temperature risen?

29. On Tuesday, the high temperature
was –10°C. On Friday, the high
temperature was 4°C. How many
degrees warmer was the high
temperature on Friday?

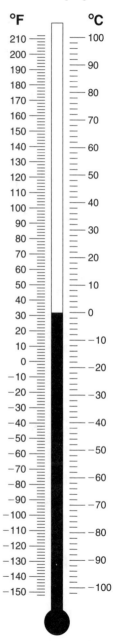

Read the scale and record the weight.

Write your answers on a separate sheet of paper.

1.

2.

3.

4.

5.

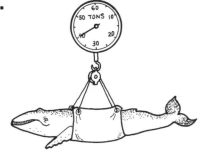

Write all of your answers on a separate sheet of paper.

Find the missing numbers. Use fractions.

1 meter = 10 decimeters	1 yard = 3 feet
1 meter = 100 centimeters	1 yard = 36 inches
1 decimeter = 10 centimeters	1 foot = 12 inches
1 centimeter = 10 millimeters	

Example   3 centimeters = ■ meter

  3 centimeters = $\frac{3}{100}$ meter

6. 1 inch = ■ foot

7. ■ meter = 1 centimeter

8. 1 foot = ■ yard

9. ■ decimeter = 1 centimeter

10. ■ meter = 1 decimeter

11. 6 centimeters = ■ meter

12. 12 inches = ■ foot

13. ■ centimeter = 1 millimeter

14. 2 feet = ■ yard

15. 70 centimeters = ■ meter

16. ■ yard = 24 inches

17. 9 decimeters = ■ meter

Find the factors for each number listed below.

> *The factors of a number* are the numbers that can be multiplied by whole numbers to get that number or the numbers that a number can be divided by without having remainders.

18. 9

19. 20

20. 35

21. 60

22. 8

23. 51

24. 32

25. 45

26. 21

Write all of your answers on a separate sheet of paper.

Tell which unit you would use to measure each item. Choose from gallon, quart, pint, cup, ounce, and tablespoon.

1. amount of water you drink with dinner

2. container of milk that you buy at the store

3. amount of water in a bathtub

4. amount of juice in a can from a vending machine

5. amount of syrup on pancakes

6. container of orange juice that you buy at the store

7. amount of water in an eyedropper

8. amount of water in a swimming pool

9. amount of cream in a cup of coffee

10. amount of lemonade needed to serve 4 people

Solve each problem.
Circle the square products.

Unit
African lions

11. 9 × 9   **12.** 8 × 7

13. 6 × 8   **14.** 9 × 6

15. 7 × 7   **16.** 8 × 9

17. 7 × 6   **18.** 8 × 8   **19.** 7 × 9

20. 400 [800s]   **21.** 100 [700s]   **22.** 200 [500s]

Write all of your answers on a separate sheet of paper.

Find the mean for each data set below.

Example 9 5 7 6 3

Step 1 Find the total of the numbers in the data set.
$9 + 5 + 7 + 6 + 3 = 30$

Step 2 Count the numbers in the data set.
There are 5 numbers in all.

Step 3 Divide the total by 5.
$30 \div 5 = 6$
The mean is 6.

---

1. 7 2 5 6

2. 5 4 2 5 6 2

3. 12 8 7 10 13

4. 9 5 6 10 10 11 12

Find each missing number.

1 mile (mi)	=	1,760 yards (yd)
1 mile (mi)	=	5,280 feet (ft)
1 yard (yd)	=	3 feet (ft)
1 yard (yd)	=	36 inches (in.)
1 foot (ft)	=	12 inches (in.)

5. ■ feet = 2 yards

6. 18 inches = ■ ft ■ in.

7. 3 yd 2 ft = ■ ft

8. 9 ft = ■ yd ■ in.

9. 2 miles = ■ yards

10. 10,560 feet = ■ miles

11. 75 in. = ■ yd ■ in.

12. 3 ft 9 in. = ■ in.

13. 5,500 ft = ■ mi ■ ft

14. 15 ft = ■ yd

Use the bar graph to answer each question below. (Write your answers on a separate sheet of paper.)

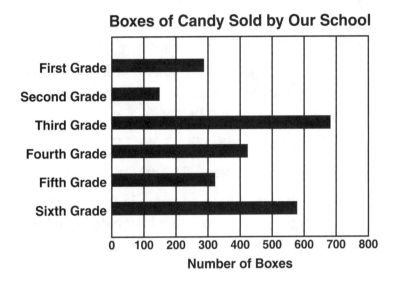

Boxes of Candy Sold by Our School

Number of Boxes

15. Which grade sold the fewest boxes of candy?

16. Which grade sold the most boxes of candy?

17. What is the range, or difference, between the highest and lowest numbers on the graph?

18. Which grade sold about twice as many boxes of candy as the second grade sold?

19. Put the grades in order from the grade that sold the most boxes to the grade that sold the fewest boxes.

20. How many more boxes of candy would the fourth grade have to sell in order to reach 500 boxes?

Find the median and the mean for each data set below. (Write your answers on a separate sheet of paper.)

Example   58, 63, 65, 49, 53, 65, 58, 72, 65, 61

To find the **median,** put the numbers in order from least to greatest. The median is the number with an equal number of values above and below it.

49, 53, 58, 58, 61, 63, 65, 65, 65, 72

The median is between 61 and 63.

To find the **mean,** add all the numbers in the data set. (*Hint:* Use a calculator.) Then count how many numbers are in the set, and divide the total by that number. Round to the nearest whole number.

58 + 63 + 65 + 49 + 53 + 65 + 58 + 72 + 65 + 61 = 609

609 ÷ 10 = 60.9

The mean is about 61.

---

1. 195, 204, 198, 187, 200, 193, 205, 187, 182

2. 929, 905, 917, 933, 904, 913, 905, 901, 908, 922

3. 397, 395, 400, 403, 397, 382, 410, 406, 395, 397

4. 1,111; 1,083; 1,102; 1,075; 1,096; 1,114; 1,111; 1,075

5. 15,270; 15,400; 15,230; 15,320; 15,290; 15,405; 15,300; 15,240; 15,320

Write all of your answers on a separate sheet of paper.

Match each measurement in the first list with an equal measurement in the second list. Write the letter that identifies that equal measurement.

> 1 gallon = 4 quarts
> 1 quart = 2 pints
> 1 pint = 2 cups
> 1 cup = 8 fluid ounces

6. 2 gallons

7. 5 cups

8. 4 fluid ounces

9. $2\frac{1}{2}$ pints

10. $\frac{1}{2}$ gallon

11. 3 pints

12. 3 quarts

13. $1\frac{1}{2}$ gallons

14. 3 cups

15. 1 cup

A. 4 pints

B. $\frac{1}{16}$ gallon

C. 24 fluid ounces

D. 6 pints

E. 5 cups

F. $\frac{1}{2}$ cup

G. 6 quarts

H. 8 quarts

I. 40 fluid ounces

J. 6 cups

Write the value of the underlined digit in each number.

16. 479,214

17. 289.46

18. 78,432

19. 3.289

20. 108.27

21. 129,568

22. 1,045,618

23. 157,214

24. 40.671

25. 357,490

26. 2,046.03

27. 92,491.045

Practice Set 75

Write all of your answers on a separate sheet of paper.

The frequency table below shows the number of boxes of cards sold by the third grade to raise money for the school library. Use a calculator to help you answer each question.

Number of Children	Number of Boxes Sold
1	~~HHT~~ ~~HHT~~ ~~HHT~~ ~~HHT~~
2	~~HHT~~ ~~HHT~~ //
3	~~HHT~~ ///
4	~~HHT~~ //
5	~~HHT~~ ~~HHT~~
6	~~HHT~~ /
7	~~HHT~~
8	////

1. What is the total number of children who sold cards?

2. How many boxes of cards were sold in all?

3. Find the **mode**, or the number that occurs most often, of the number of boxes of cards sold.

4. Find the **median** number of boxes of cards sold.

5. Find the **mean** number of boxes of cards sold.

Solve each problem.

6. Jason had 25 quarters. He put 7 of them in his bank. What fraction of the quarters did Jason put in his bank?

7. Becky spends 5 hours each day at school. What fraction of the day does Becky spend at school? (*Hint:* A day has 24 hours.)

8. Bryan has 4 history videos, 5 science videos, and 3 adventure videos. What fraction of his videos are history? What fraction of his videos are adventure?

Use with or after Lesson 10.10.

Write all of your answers on a separate sheet of paper.

Draw and shade shapes to show each fraction.

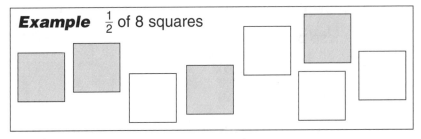

Example $\frac{1}{2}$ of 8 squares

9. $\frac{1}{4}$ of 4 triangles   **10.** $\frac{1}{3}$ of 6 circles

11. $\frac{3}{4}$ of 8 rectangles   **12.** $\frac{1}{2}$ of 10 diamonds

13. $\frac{2}{3}$ of 6 triangles   **14.** $\frac{1}{4}$ of 8 circles

---

Solve each problem.

15. Felix is following a recipe that calls for 3 cups of milk. How many cups of milk does he need to double the recipe?

16. Sharon bought 3 gallons of juice. There are 4 quarts in 1 gallon. How many quarts of juice did Sharon buy?

17. At the end of the school year, Lisa weighed 62 pounds. She had gained 6 pounds during the school year. How much did Lisa weigh at the beginning of school?

18. Sarah rode her bike 18 kilometers Monday and 25 kilometers Tuesday. How many kilometers did she ride her bike in all those two days?

19. A garden in the shape of a square measures 3 meters on each side. How many meters of fencing would you need to put fencing around the entire garden?

Write all of your answers on a separate sheet of paper.

Draw the following grid on cm grid paper.
Then follow the directions.

1. Plot these points:

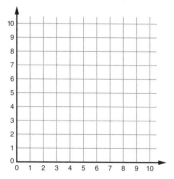

A: (1,1)	*B:* (3,6)
C: (6,3)	*D:* (7,0)
E: (5,6)	*F:* (7,9)
G: (10,6)	*H:* (3,9)

2. Draw the following line segments: $\overline{AB}, \overline{BC}, \overline{CA}$
What shape did you make?

3. Draw the following line segments: $\overline{DE}, \overline{EF}, \overline{FG}, \overline{GD}$
What shape did you make?

4. Which shape is symmetrical?

5. Measure the following line segments
to the nearest centimeter: $\overline{AB}, \overline{DG}, \overline{FG}, \overline{CE}$

Find the volume of each box.
Each cube stands for 1 cubic inch.

6.

7.

8.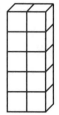

9.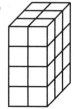

Write all of your answers on a separate sheet of paper.

Imagine that each of the following containers is tipped over onto a table.

1.

500 Pennies

How many HEADS? How many TAILS?

2.

200 counters

How many *black* sides faceup?
How many *white* sides faceup?

3.

50 buttons

How many *front* sides faceup?
How many *back* sides faceup?

Solve each division problem. If the problem has a remainder, write that amount after the letter *R*.

Example $100 \div 9 \rightarrow 11$ R1

4. $81 \div 9$ **5.** $54 \div 6$ **6.** $72 \div 8$

7. $56 \div 8$ **8.** $48 \div 6$ **9.** $36 \div 6$

10. $35 \div 4$ **11.** $200 \div 6$ **12.** $95 \div 4$

13. $17 \div 6$ **14.** $3,000 \div 5$ **15.** $332 \div 10$

Write all of your answers on a separate sheet of paper.

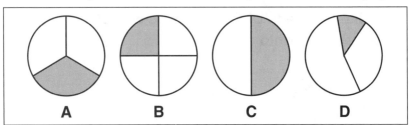

A   B   C   D

On which of the spinners above ...

1. are you equally likely to land on the shaded part or the white part?

2. are you likely to land on the shaded part about $\frac{1}{4}$ of the time?

3. are you twice as likely to land on a white part?

4. are you likely to land on a white part about $\frac{3}{4}$ of the time?

5. are you likely to land on the shaded part about $\frac{1}{3}$ of the time?

Find the mean of each data set below.

> *To find the mean,* add all the numbers in the data set. Then count how many numbers are in the set, and divide the total by that number. Round to the nearest whole number.

6. 349, 756, 821, 444, 348, 259

7. 3,500; 3,511; 3,487; 3,548

8. 28, 34, 56, 54, 76, 89, 21, 13, 49, 112

9. 1,001; 1,012; 998; 799; 804; 1,030

Write the missing numbers on a separate sheet of paper.

10.

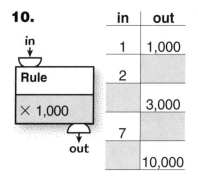

in	out
1	1,000
2	
	3,000
7	
	10,000

Rule
× 1,000

11.

in	out
1	16
	32
	64
7	
	160

Rule
× 16

12.

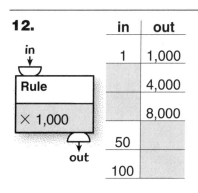

in	out
1	1,000
	4,000
	8,000
50	
100	

Rule
× 1,000

13.

in	out
1	2,000
2	
4	
	20,000
7	

Rule
× 2,000

**Make the following predictions
on a separate sheet of paper:**

1. You make 10 random draws. *You draw ...*
- blue 4 times
- red 4 times
- yellow 2 times

5 blocks inside

Predict the colors of the 5 blocks in the bag.
Tell what fraction of the blocks are NOT yellow.

2. You make 25 random draws. *You draw ...*
- orange 16 times
- purple 9 times

Predict the colors of the 5 blocks in the bag.

3. You make 50 random draws. *You draw ...*
- red 19 times
- blue 21 times
- white 10 times

Predict the colors of the 5 blocks in the bag.
Tell what fraction of the blocks are white.

4. You make 50 random draws. *You draw ...*
- blue 26 times
- red 24 times

6 blocks inside

Predict the colors of the 6 blocks in the bag.

5. You make 40 random draws. *You draw ...*
- pink 6 times
- orange 13 times
- red 7 times
- green 14 times

Predict the colors of the 6 blocks in the bag.
Tell what fraction of the blocks are pink.

Find the missing number for each Fact Triangle.
Then write the number family for that triangle. (Write
your answers on a separate sheet of paper.)

Example   Missing number: 9

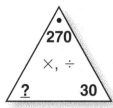

$9 \times 30 = 270$

$30 \times 9 = 270$

$270 \div 9 = 30$

$270 \div 30 = 9$

6.
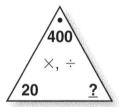

7.

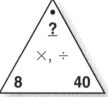

8.
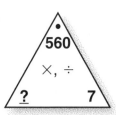

9.
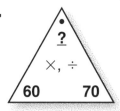

10.
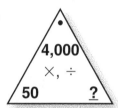

11.
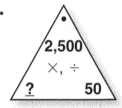

Practice Set 80

Copy the chart below onto another sheet of paper.
Then add numbers to the chart and find the total
for each column. Then answer the questions.

There are 5 third grade classes at Lincoln Elementary.
- Room 101 has 12 boys and 12 girls.
- Room 102 has 14 boys and 12 girls.
- Room 103 has 13 boys and 13 girls.
- Room 104 has 11 boys and 13 girls.
- Room 105 has 12 boys and 11 girls.

1. **Number of Third Graders at
Lincoln Elementary School**

Room Number	Boys	Girls
101		
102		
103		
104		
105		
TOTALS		

2. Use fractions to tell about how many of the third grade
students are girls and about how many are boys.

3. There are about 100 *second* graders at the school.
Predict how many are boys and how many are girls.

4. There are about 130 *fourth* graders at the school.
Predict how many are girls and how many are boys.

5. Can you predict whether a new student in the third
grade will be a boy or a girl?

Use with or after Lesson 11.7.